Our Ever-Changing Coasts

Written by:

Peter Hancock

First published
September 06 in Great Britain by

e PRINT

Educational Printing Services Limited
Albion Mill, Water Street, Great Harwood, Blackburn BB6 7QR
Telephone: (01254) 882080   Fax: (01254) 882010
E-mail: enquiries@eprint.co.uk   Website: www.eprint.co.uk

ISBN 1 904904 97 1

Contents

Teachers' Notes

The aim of this volume is to provide an up-to-date resource for the teaching of the geography of our coasts. Each chapter begins with an overview of a particular topic, supported by maps and diagrams, and is followed by a topical case study. The book can be used as the core text for the study of coasts, or individual chapters or case studies may be selected to support other work.

The majority of examples are based on the UK, but the final chapter provides a broader picture, with a case study of international concern, as well as work based on global location.

Pupils' tasks are divided between written work, marked ∿ and practical activities, marked ℗. Written work is differentiated, so that the level of work may be set according to individual pupils' abilities. It is left to the teacher's discretion as to whether the pupils are informed of this difference, but they are coded as follows:

Easier tasks that may be undertaken by the majority of pupils are labelled Trickle

Harder tasks, or ones that require more research, are called Splash S

More challenging work is denoted Deluge D

Introduction

The British Isles is made up of some 6,000 islands, some large, some very small. In total there is nearly 12,000 kms of coastline. As an island race Britain has always been influenced by the sea and her coasts. It has been the sea that has helped shape our history; from across the English Channel (but known as La Manche by the French) came Roman and later Norman invaders, while the same sea helped repel invasions from Napoleonic France and Hitler's Germany during World War Two. The sea provided Britain with the chance to become a great naval power and establish an empire spanning the globe, it provided an opportunity for trade, fishing and more recently the search for oil and gas far beneath the surface.

We refer to the coast'line', yet it is a line that is constantly changing. As the meeting point between land and sea it is subject to constant erosion and deposition. Some stretches of coastline are more able to stand up to the onslaught of the waves than others; tall granite cliffs appear immovable while low salt marshes may be inundated regularly by the sea. Such areas may require sea defences to be built to protect places inland.

Vast amounts of energy are released when the sea is whipped up into waves by the wind, or is spent against the intransigent cliffs. It is an energy source that, at the moment, has huge potential but has yet to be harnessed in any significant way. However, it still forms a source of enjoyment for a large number of people participating in water sports, from professional sailors to children playing with model boats.

Locations of Case Studies

Norfolk
Broads

Severn
Bore

Essex Marshes

Thames Barrier

West Sussex
Coast

Port of Dover

Beachy Head

St. Piran's Church

Chesil Beach
and Jurassic Coast

Fal Estuary

Chapter One

Waves and Wave Action

The Formation of Breakers

The wind may blow across a large expanse of sea or ocean before reaching land. The distance over which the wind blows is known as the **fetch**. As wind disturbs the surface of the ocean, waves are formed which may increase in size for as long as the wind blows, so the larger the fetch, the bigger the waves that can be created.

Beneath the surface the water moves in a circular motion (Figure 1). As soon as the waves reach a shore this movement is disrupted as the circle `bottoms out` on the sand, forcing the circle into an oval. On the surface the wave will start to curl into a breaking wave.

Figure 1

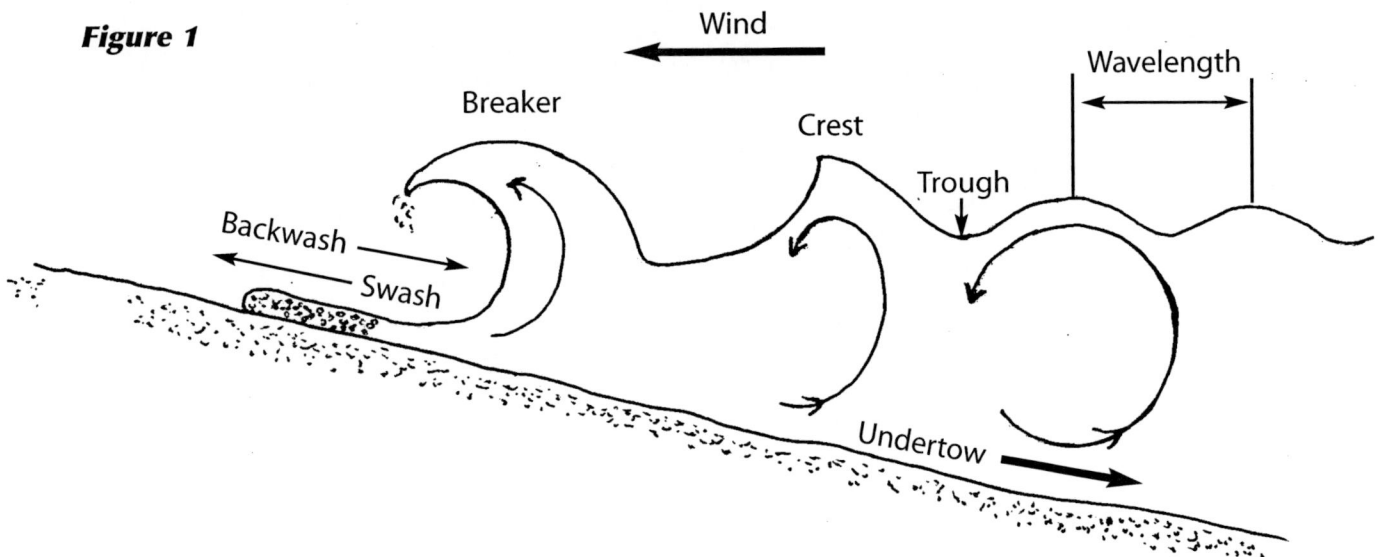

The size and shape of the wave will depend upon the strength and direction of the wind and the gradient of the sea shore (Figure 2). These factors will influence whether they are **destructive** or **constructive** waves. Once the wave has broken, white foam called **swash** or **uprush** flows up the beach. This water returns as **backwash**, dragging sand and pebbles with it.

Figure 2

Types of Waves

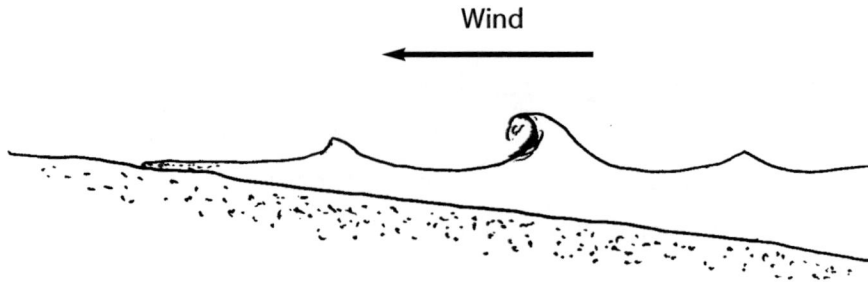

Wind

A flat or gentle slope will cause the wave to break before it reaches the shore.

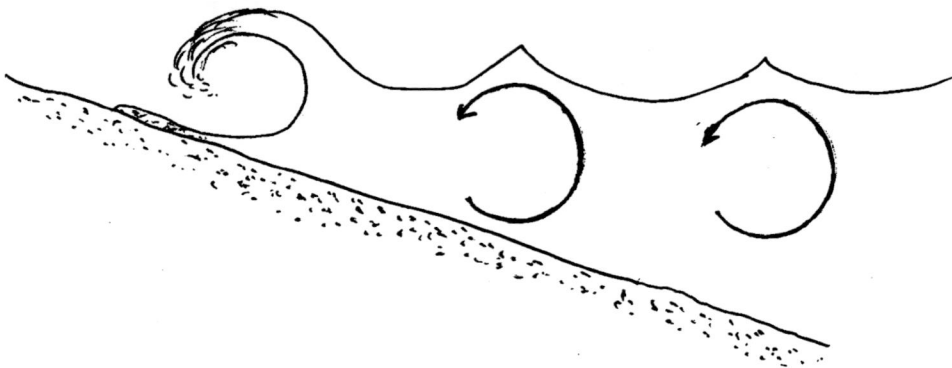

On a sloping beach the waves break late and crash against the shore. (These are sometimes referred to as `dumpers` by surfers.)

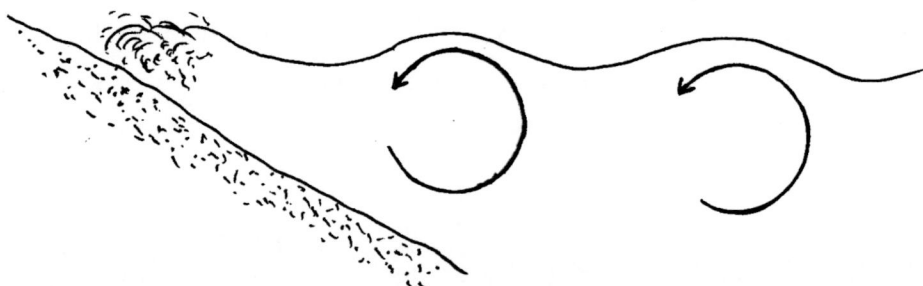

If the shore is very steep the waves will not have the opportunity to form breakers, but will surge against the shoreline.

1. Which would have the larger fetch, the North Sea or Pacific Ocean?

2. What will the swash and backwash do to the sand and pebbles?

3. (a) Look at Figure 1. Explain how the undertow is formed.

   (b) Why may the undertow be dangerous to swimmers?

4. (a) Look at Figure 2. Using your own words explain how each type of wave is formed.

   (b) Which would be the better surf wave? Why?

Destructive Waves

These erode the coast, for as the wave crashes onto the shore they wear away loose or soft rock and remove sand. This is then dragged out to sea by the backwash. This can present real problems:

(a) beaches are a natural defensive barrier and help protect the land behind from attack by the sea.

(b) Beaches are an important attraction in many places, and are vital to the tourist industry.

(c) The sand and shingle above the high water mark forms a natural habitat for many species of plants and are important to nature conservation.

Figure 3

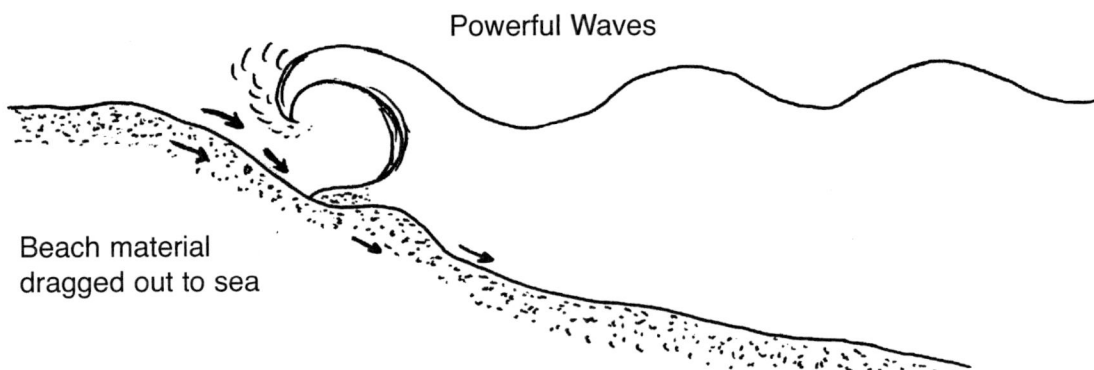

Powerful Waves

Beach material dragged out to sea

Constructive Waves

Gently breaking waves may push more material up the beach, and as they are slow and have lost their energy, the load they have been carrying is dropped.

Figure 4

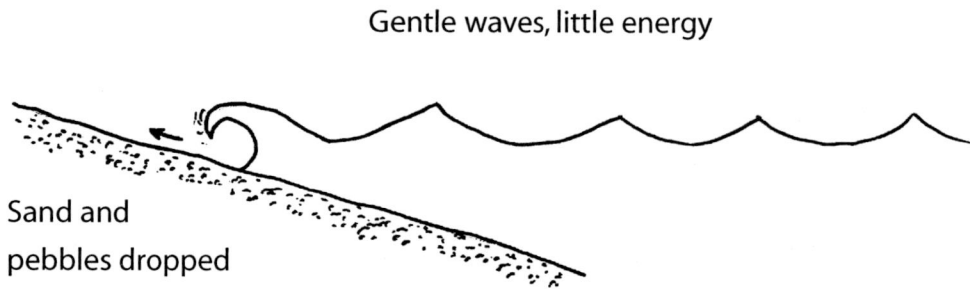

Gentle waves, little energy

Sand and
pebbles dropped

Whether a wave is destructive or constructive depends on the balance between the uprush and the backwash (Figure 5).

Figure 5

Constructive

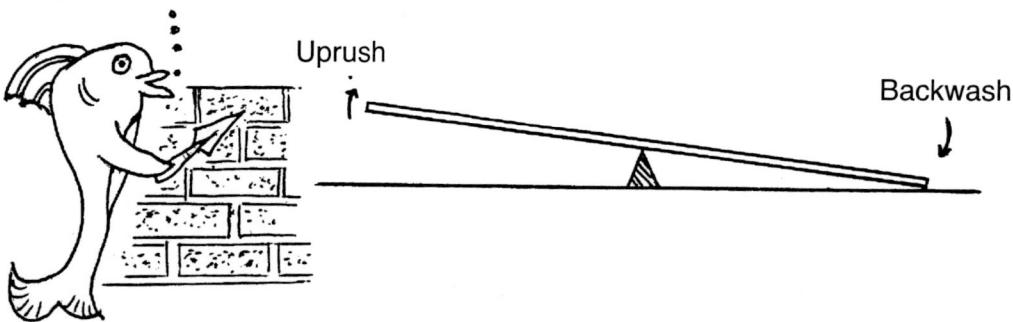

Uprush

Backwash

Destructive

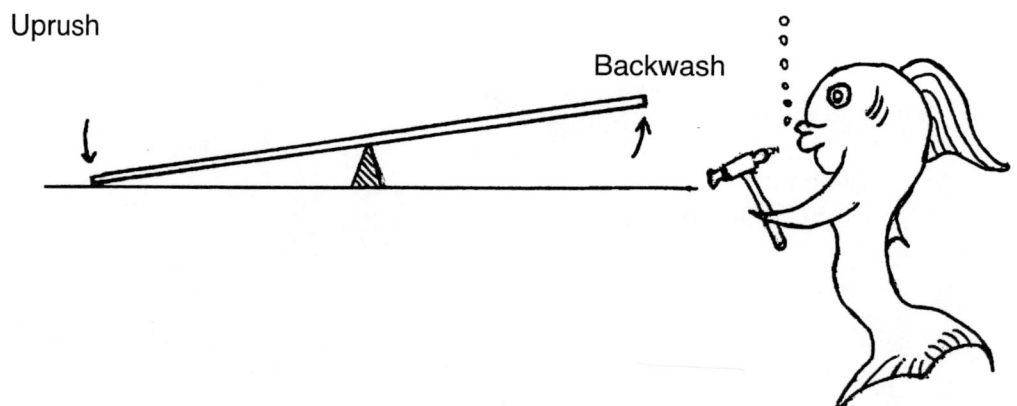

Uprush

Backwash

Tides

   Unlike rivers and lakes, the shoreline is affected by the ebb and flow of the tides. This twice-daily rise and fall is created by the gravitational pull of the moon. The part of the earth nearest the moon will experience high tide as the gravity of the moon draws the water towards it. On the other side of the earth a low tide will occur.

Figure 6

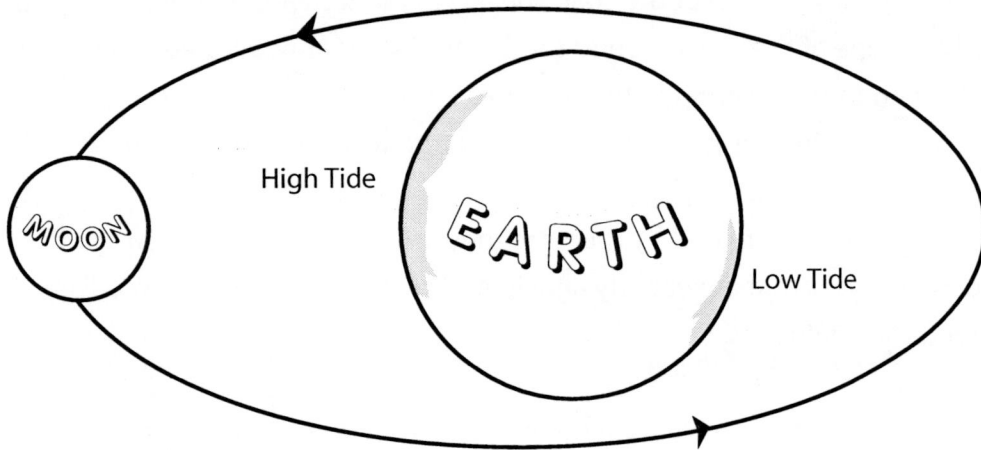

   Spring tides occur when the sun, moon and earth align (are in syzygy), causing the attraction to be multiplied.

   Neap tides see the attraction reduced when the Sun and Moon form a right angle (in quadrature). This is a period of the lowest tidal movement.

   Many animals and plants depend on the rise and fall of the sea level for their survival. Some creatures, such as crabs, have adapted to breathe in air and water in order to survive on the shoreline.

Case Study - The Severn Bore

As has been seen, the distance the sea rises and falls is not constant. The Severn Estuary has the second highest tide in the world, after the Bay of Fundy in Canada. The difference between the highest and lowest tide can be as much as 15 metres in a single day. The River Severn is also the longest river in Britain, flowing for 350 km from its source at Plynlimon in Wales before draining into the Bristol Channel.

The topography (shape) of the coastline will influence what happens as the tide changes. The shape of the coast around the Severn Estuary has created a natural funnel that gets narrower and shallower. So as the tide rises in the Bristol Channel the water is channelled into this decreasing space, causing a large wave or bore to form. (See Figure 7)

As these waves are created by the tides they are predictable and spring tides occur on a number of days a year that are eagerly anticipated by surfers and canoeists. The best bores occur around the equinoxes.

The Severn Bore has a maximum height of 2.8 metres and travels at an average speed of 16 km/hour. The waves move upriver past Gloucester, before being halted by the weir at Maisemore.

Figure 7

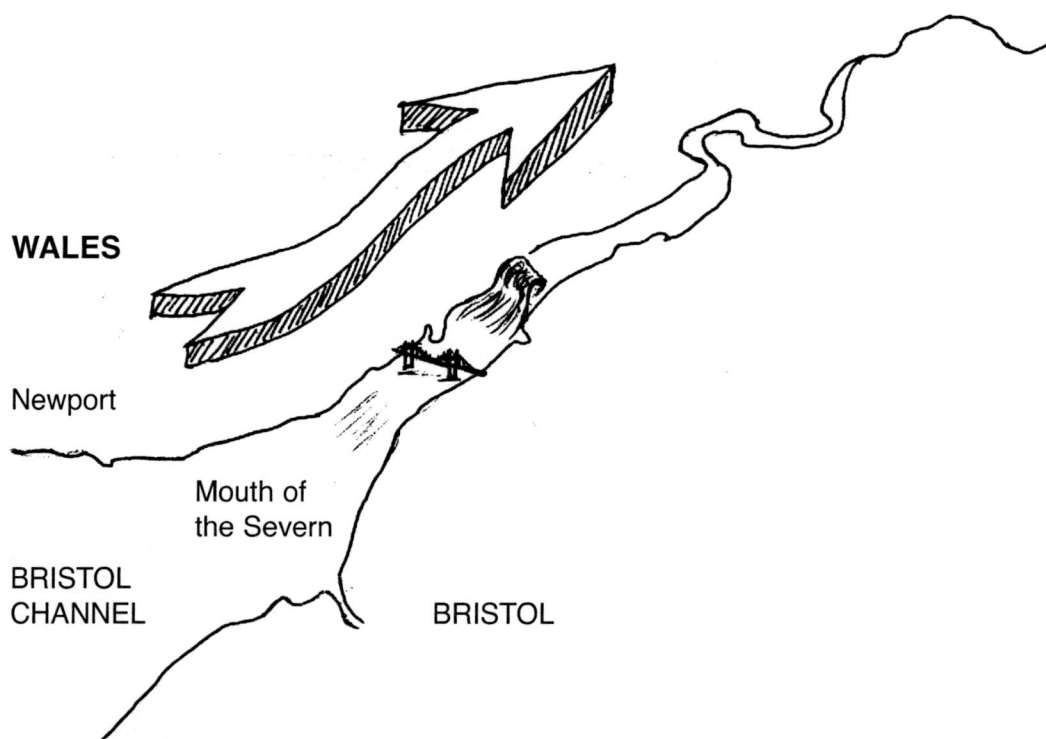

WALES

Newport

Mouth of
the Severn

BRISTOL
CHANNEL

BRISTOL

5. Some 60 bores occur throughout the world - including eight in the UK - where there are similar conditions to those found in the Severn Estuary. Others occur on the rivers Seine and Gironde in France, the Amazon in Brazil and the Indus and Brahmaputra in India. Try to find out more about another bore.

6. The highest tides in continental Europe occur at Mont Saint Michel in France where there is up to 15 metres difference between low and high water. Try to find out more about the geography of this area and the dangers these tidal extremes can create.

7. Fill in the spaces on Figure 8 below. Only refer to Figure 1 if you have to.

Figure 8

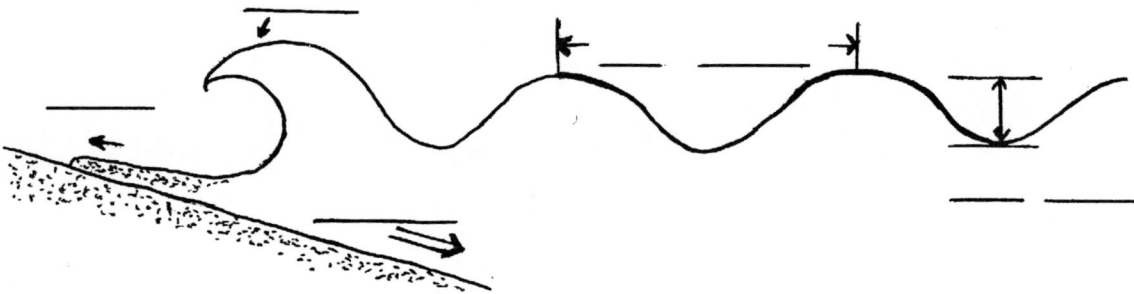

8. During a field trip to a beach collect sand samples at different locations, and plot their positions on a sketch map. Back at school these can be organised in a sand tray, a box divided into compartments. Considering the colour of the sand, the texture and size of grains, find different types of sand to put in each compartment.

Links with Science

9. During your field trip conduct a belt transect experiment. Use a quadrat to identify various species along a stretch of coast. A chart or book to help you identify them may be useful. You might find crabs, mussels, serrated wrack, sea lettuce, limpets, periwinkles, barnacles - who knows? Your results could be compared with those taken from other beaches or at different times of the year.

10. Try making a plaster cast of different footprints in the wet sand. Use a ring of card to contain the wet plaster. Again, try to identify the species.

Chapter Two

Coastal Erosion

Erosion means the wearing away of rocks. The sea is a very good agent of this, and is able to do so through a number of **processes**, outlined below:

Abrasion

Waves throw pebbles and rocks against the cliffs, causing them and the cliff to be worn away. In particular this takes place during stormy weather, when the waves are capable of hurling rocks weighing several tonnes.

Attrition

Rocks and pebbles collide into each other, becoming smaller and rounder. Eventually the particles form sand.

Corrosion

Salt and chemicals in the sea water dissolve some rocks such as limestone and chalk.

Hydraulic Action

As the waves crash against the cliffs, air is trapped in cracks and compressed. Air is forced further into crevasses. As it is released by the retreating wave it draws out loose stones.

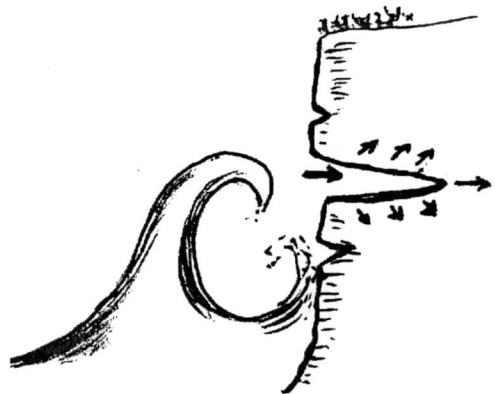

Transportation

The eroded material may be moved along the coast as the result of the action of waves, such as **longshore drift** (See Chapter 3).

Rates of Coastal Erosion

The speed at which the coast may be eroded depends on a number of factors, as shown in the diagram below:

Figure 1

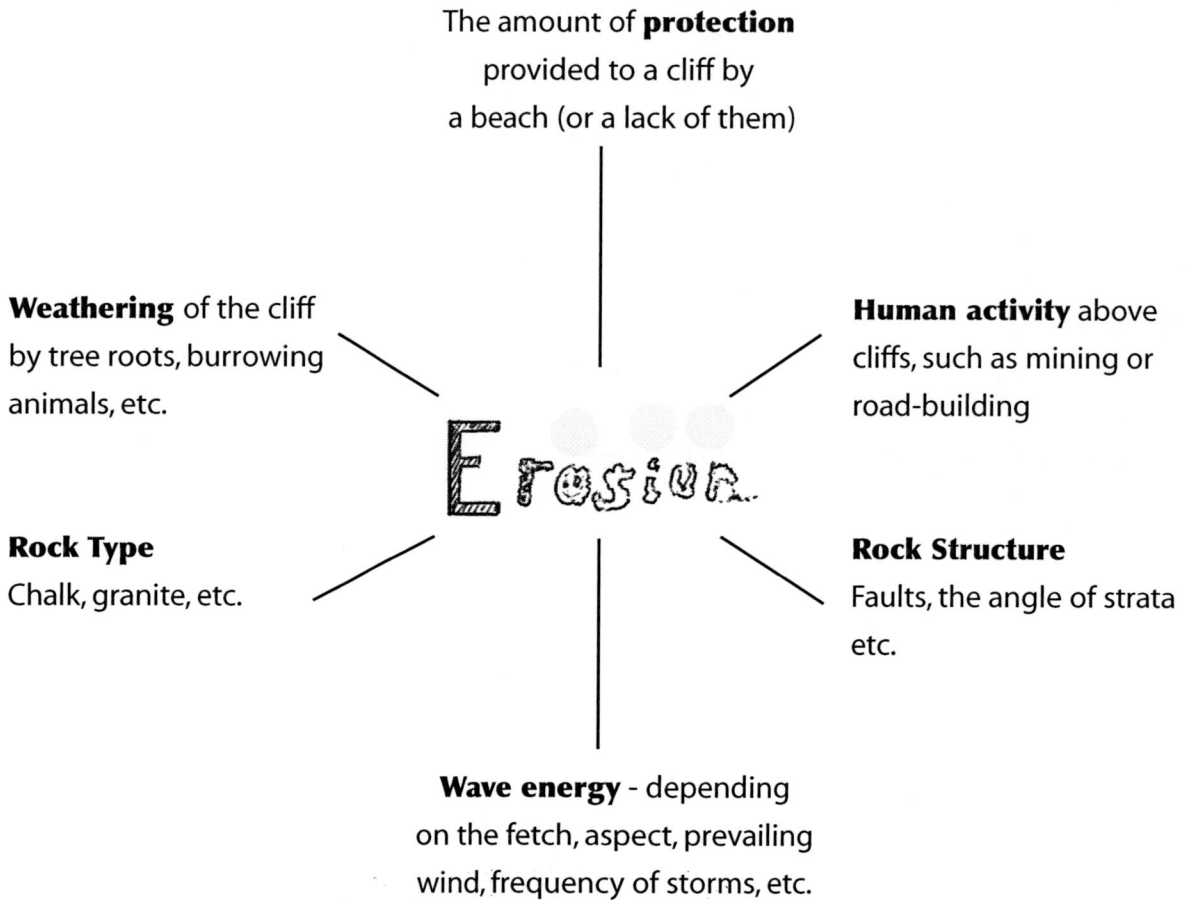

The amount of **protection** provided to a cliff by a beach (or a lack of them)

Weathering of the cliff by tree roots, burrowing animals, etc.

Human activity above cliffs, such as mining or road-building

Rock Type
Chalk, granite, etc.

Rock Structure
Faults, the angle of strata etc.

Wave energy - depending on the fetch, aspect, prevailing wind, frequency of storms, etc.

Features Created By Coastal Erosion

Headlands, Caves, Arches and Stacks

Figure 2

1 Headland

2 Fault Cave

3 Blowhole Lintel Arch

4 Stack Stump

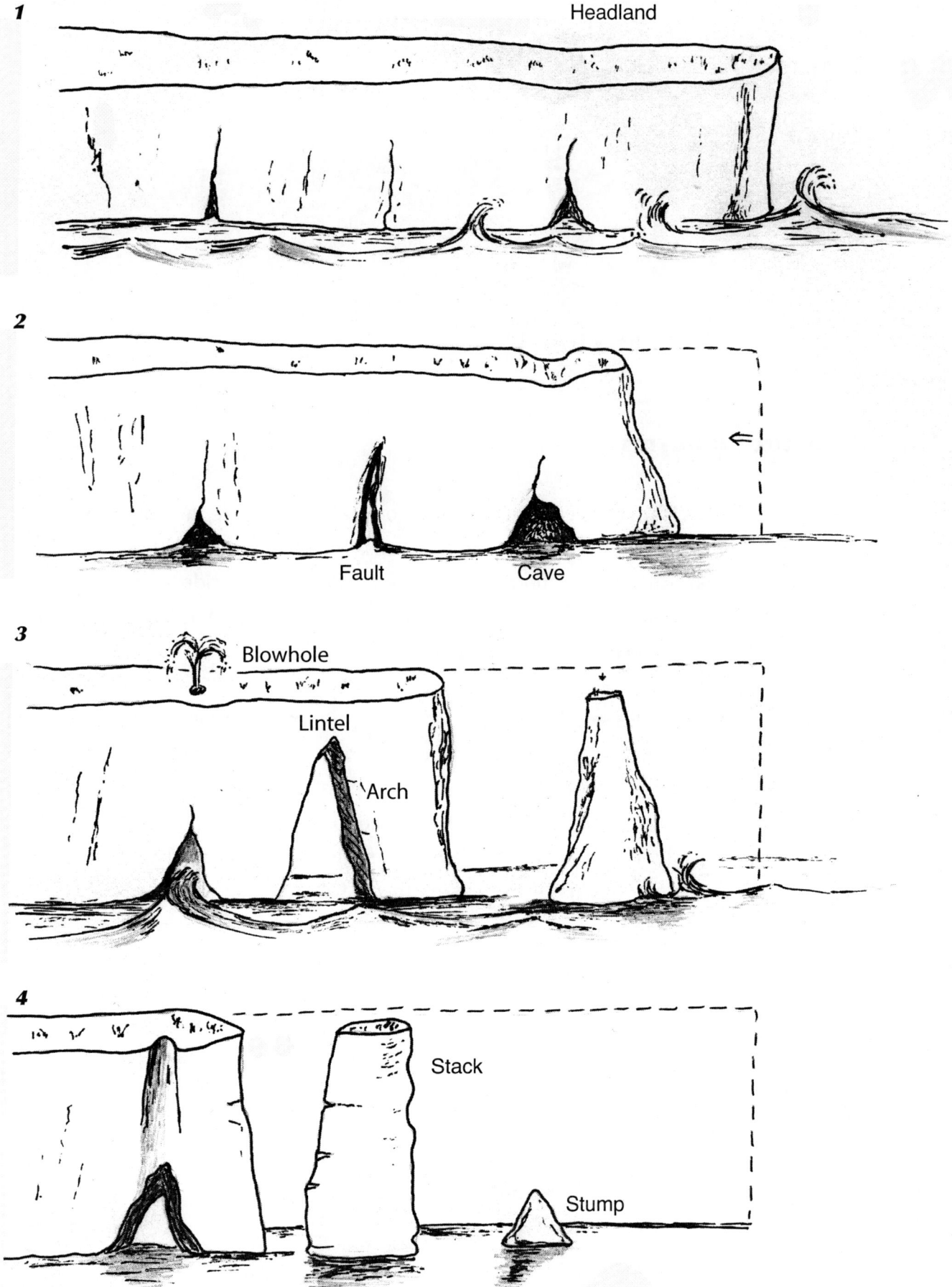

Notches

These are often formed at the foot of cliffs, for the greatest amount of erosion occurs a little further up the cliff from the high water mark. This is revealed by a curved indentation in the cliff known as a **notch**.

Figure 3

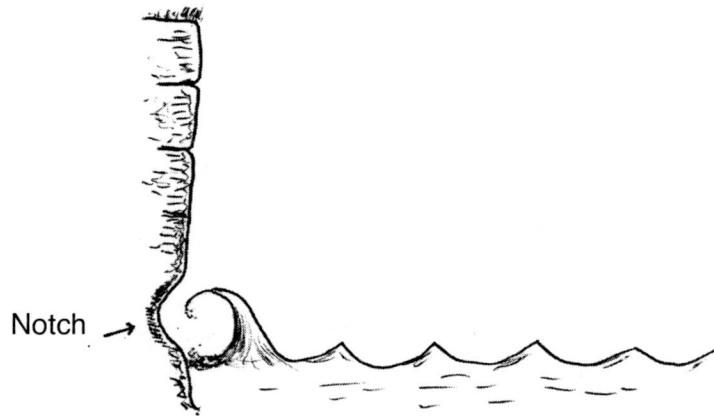

Notch →

Wave-cut Platforms

Over time the cliff may recede (be cut back): rock collapses above the notch and faults are widened and weakened, particularly during storms. This may leave a feature called a **wave-cut platform**. Here we may find rock pools left exposed at low tide in what is referred to as the **inter-tidal zone**. The wave-cut platform may grow so large that the waves rarely reach the cliff any more, so it becomes a **dead cliff**.

Rock pools provide a safe haven for a wide variety of marine organisms. There is often abundant food and the numerous cracks and crevices are good hiding places from predators. However, during storms, powerful waves may dislodge plants and animals. Some have adjusted to the conditions, such as barnacles cemented to the rocks yet able to spend several days out of water, while snails and mussels have hard shells for protection. The creatures that inhabit the rock pools also have had to adapt in other ways: on hot summer days the water temperature rises dramatically, and as water evaporates, the salt concentration increases; during heavy rains the salt water may be diluted so that it is almost fresh.

Figure 4 - Wave-cut Platform

1. **Label the diagram with:**

Notch: Wave-cut platform: Faults widened by erosion: Overhanging rock: Rock pool: Original coastline

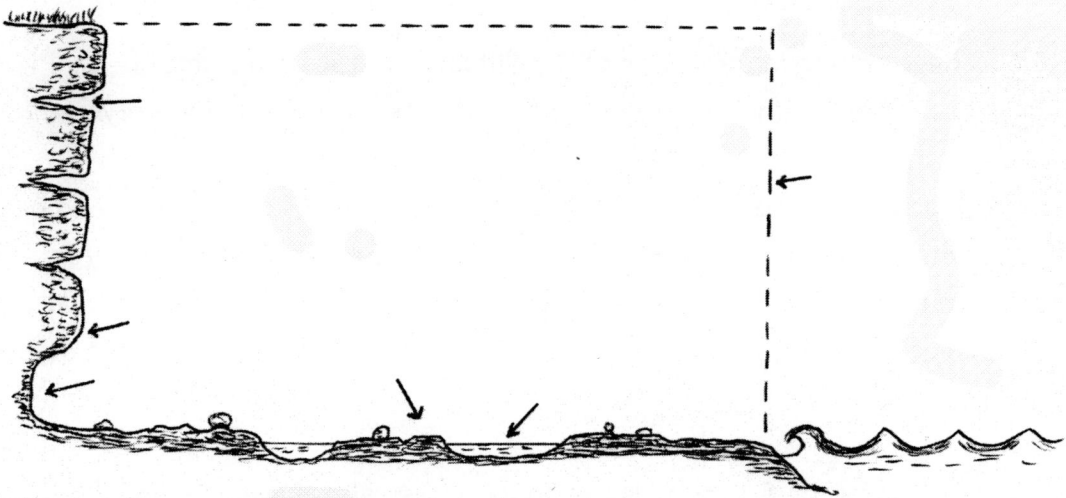

2. **Using Figure 2 to help you, copy the following, filling in the blanks:**

An area of hard rock may be e_____ less quickly than the softer rock around it, leaving a h_____. However, this may still have fissures, faults or weaknesses that will be eroded to form c_____. On rare occasions a natural tunnel may be created, forming a b_____ that allows an incoming wave to shoot up in a fountain of water.

Over time the sea may break through the back of the cave, forming an a_____. When this natural bridge or lintel collapses a column of rock called a s_____ will be left. A small stack is known as a s_____.

The rate of erosion will depend on the t_____ of rock that forms the cliff, and the power of the w_____. This in turn may be influenced by the tides, prevailing w_____ and the fetch.

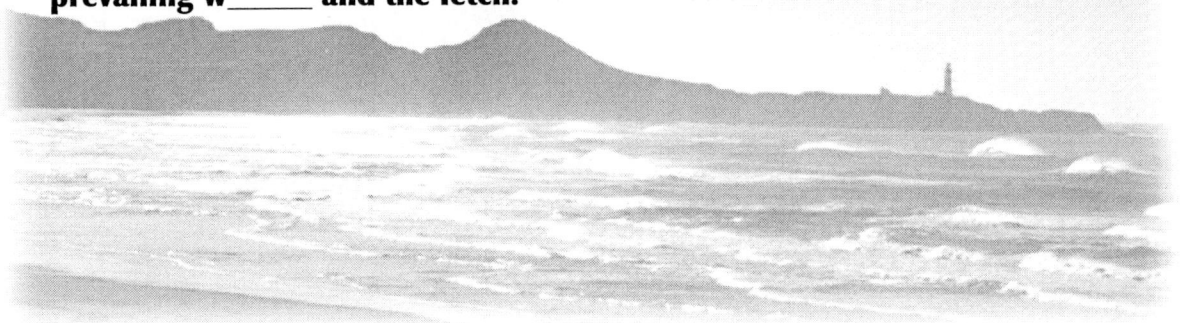

Case Study - Beachy Head

Cape Wrath on the north coast of Scotland has the highest sea cliffs in mainland Britain. Beachy Head on the south coast near Eastbourne, Sussex, boasts the highest **chalk** cliffs in the United Kingdom. However, because chalk is soft and easily eroded, the famous cliffs are losing up to a metre to the sea each year.

In January 1999 a large section of the cliff face fell 150 metres into the sea. It was described as being Britain's biggest single loss of coastline in living memory.

Previously the unmanned Beachy Head lighthouse had stood on an island beneath the cliffs, but when thousands of tonnes of rock slipped it created a causeway of rubble stretching out to the base of the tower. Few people could remember a single fall anywhere approaching this; a fifteen metre deep slab of rock had slipped across a 180 metre stretch of coast.

The reason for the fall was believed to have been above average rainfall causing water to penetrate the rock. Then in the cold weather the water froze and expanded, forcing the cliff to break up.

There are indications that such falls could become more frequent as a result of climate change. In times of drought the chalk dries out, then during periods of heavy rain the cliffs become water-logged. This puts buildings, such as houses or the nearby old Belle Toute lighthouse, at risk. Rising sea levels will also increase the rate of erosion at the base of the cliffs.

Figure 5

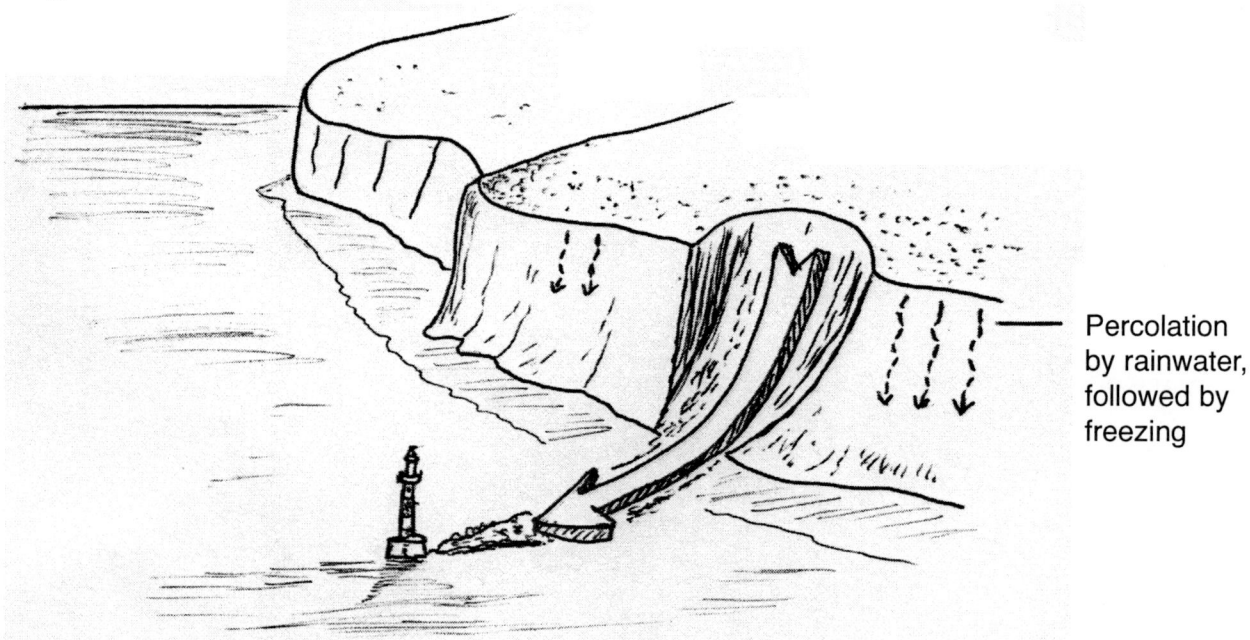

Percolation by rainwater, followed by freezing

3. Where are the highest sea cliffs in mainland Britain?

4. Which is the nearest town to Beachy Head?

5. The cliffs meet the _____ Channel and face _____.
   (North, south east or west?)

6. What important man-made feature stands at the base of the cliffs?

7. Which of the following words best describe the cliffs at Beachy Head?
   Hard: granite: limestone: porous: chalk: soft: low: impervious: tall.
   (You may find the glossary at the back of the book helpful).

8. What indications are there that large landslides such as the one described in the Case Study may become more frequent?

9. In what ways are landslides on cliffs a danger?

10. Do such landslides matter, or should we just accept them as examples of geographical change? Write down your ideas, then discuss them as a class or in small groups.

Chapter Three

Longshore Drift

As has been seen in Chapter 1, when the waves break on the shore they can move material up the beach or remove it completely. We refer to such waves as constructive or destructive.

However, if the wind blows towards the beach at an angle (obliquely), it will cause the waves to move diagonally, and so strike the beach at an angle (Figure 1).

Figure 1

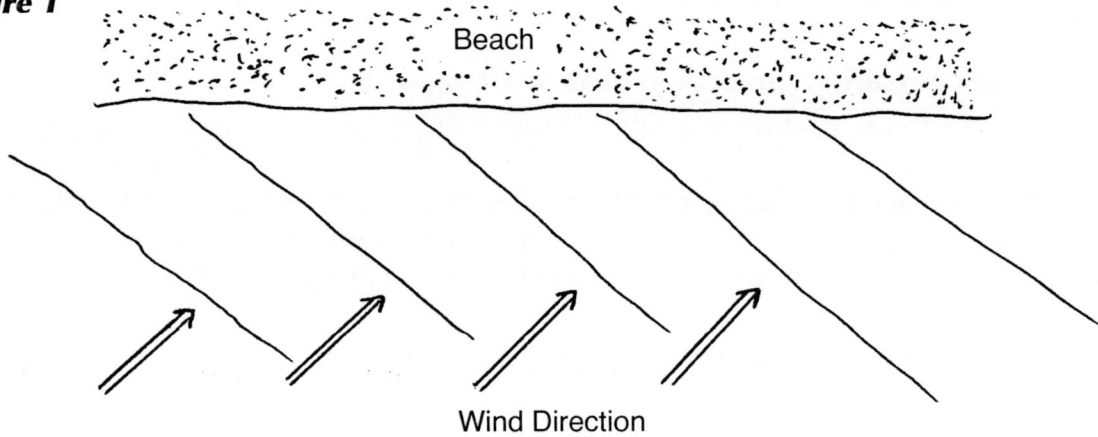

Beach

Wind Direction

As the waves move up the beach the **swash** washes sand and shingle up the slope at an angle to the shoreline, while the **backwash** drags it straight back down (Figure 2). This process is known as **longshore drift**.

Figure 2

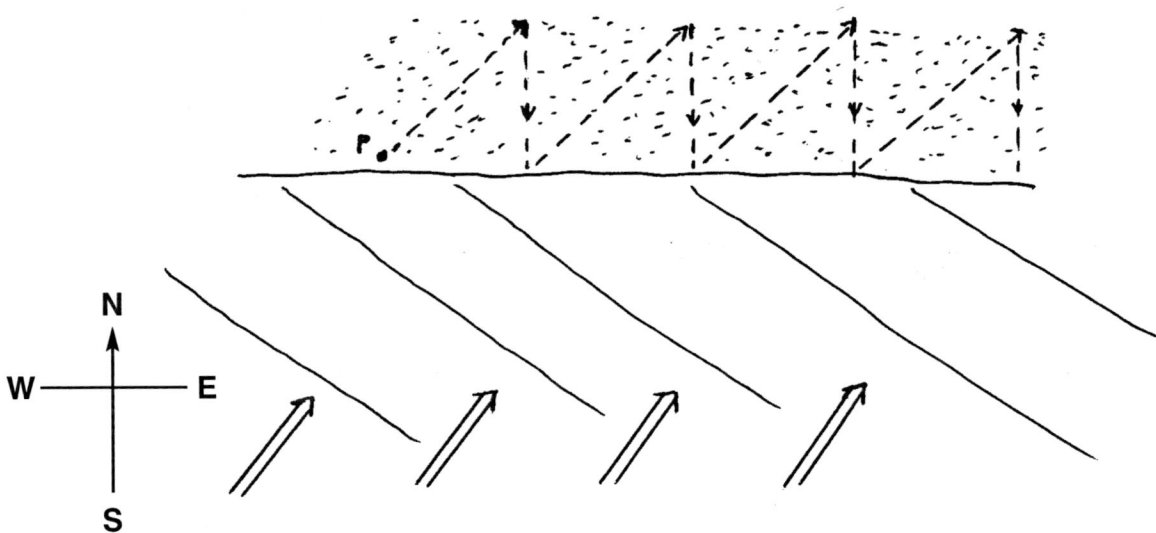

N
W — E
S

1. What is going to happen to the pebble marked P?

2. Using the compass on Figure 2, try to work out in which direction the pebble is moving.

3. What could happen naturally to stop this movement, or even reverse it?

4. Is longshore drift a process of erosion or deposition?

In areas that experience a **prevailing wind** (one that blows from one direction more often that any other) longshore drift may become a major problem. Also, if the coast continues in one direction, the problem could continue for many kilometres.

5. Why do you think longshore drift may be a problem?

6. Can you come up with a plan to stop longshore drift along a stretch of coast? Remember, it has to be a practical idea, and relatively cheap to use on a long length of coast. You can use the diagram below (Figure 3) to work out your ideas.

Figure 3

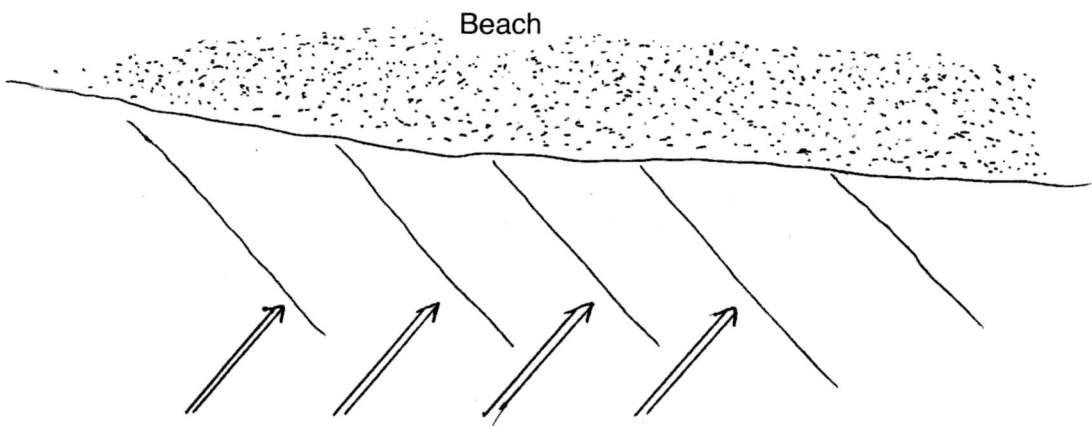

Beach

Dealing with Longshore Drift

One method that has proved to be fairly cheap and effective in reducing the amount of beach material being removed is to construct wooden, or occasionally concrete, barriers stretching out from the beach (Figure 4). Such barriers are known as **groynes**. These interfere with the diagonal movement of the waves as they approach the shore and help prevent sand being moved too far down the beach.

Figure 4

Groynes

Wind

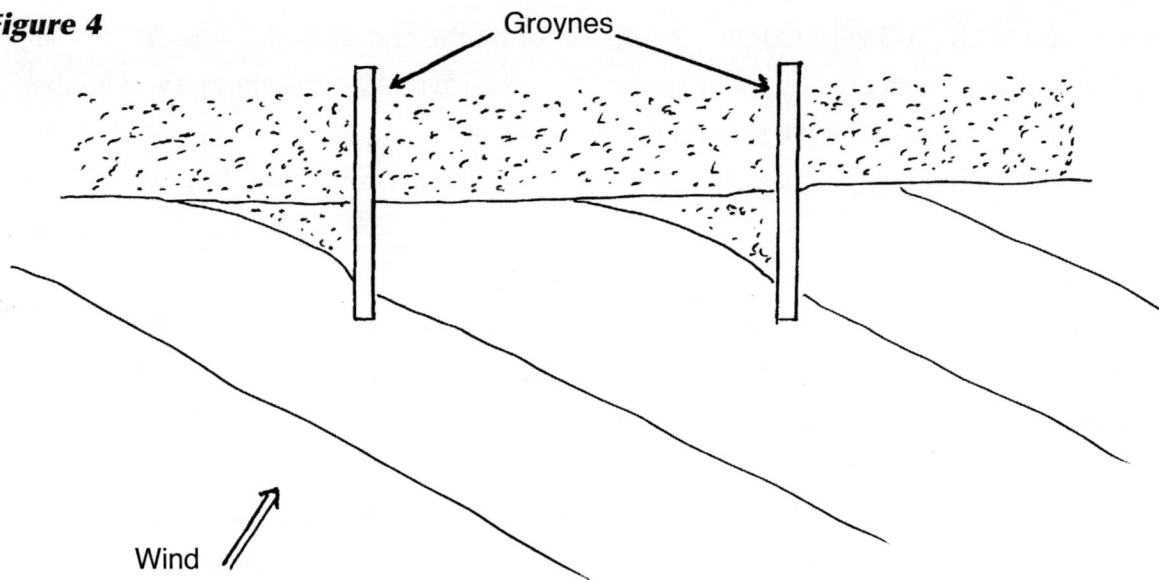

S 7.   Look at an ordnance survey map of the south coast, such as in West Sussex in the case study below. Can you identify any groynes?

P 8.   You may find groynes on a stretch of coast near you. Try to measure the distance between the groynes along a stretch of coast. Is the distance constant, or does it depend on coastal conditions?

How effective are they at stopping longshore drift?

Case Study - The West Sussex Coast

In some areas of the British Isles long stretches of coastline are subjected to longshore drift, and the shore has to be protected by many kilometres of groynes. These are a prominent feature along the West Sussex coast and beyond.

It is likely that the shingle that forms the beaches of this coast were originally washed down from the South Downs to low-lying areas during the end of the Ice Age. When the English Channel was created by rising sea levels as the ice melted, the shingle was washed ashore creating the beaches we see today. Now they are being reduced by coastal erosion. As the shingle is not being replenished, there are growing concerns that they may not be **sustainable**.

As a result of prevailing winds the sand and shingle is being moved eastwards along the coast. To interfere with this groynes now stretch out into the sea on many of the beaches, such as those at Worthing (A on Figure 5).

At Shoreham (B) it has been estimated that about 15,000 cubic metres of shingle a year ends up at the eastern end of Shoreham beach where it is finally stopped by the western breakwater. At Shoreham Port a process known as shingle bypassing has been adopted. During the spring and autumn shingle is removed from the west side of the harbour entrance and transported to the east side. A similar problem exists at Kingston Beach where again there is a movement of shingle from west to east that can threaten the A259 Brighton to Worthing road. So, every four or five years when there is a shortage of shingle at the western end, `shingle recycling operations` take place, and it is returned from further eastwards up the coast.

Other problems have beset Brighton's sea front and its famous Victorian piers (C). The West Pier was closed to the public in 1975. Then in January 2003 part of the pier collapsed into the sea. It now needs renovating: this would be very expensive, but the longer it is left the more acute the problems become. Then on 5 February 2003 the famous Brighton Pier (formerly the Palace Pier) caught fire, but fortunately has been restored.

Figure 5

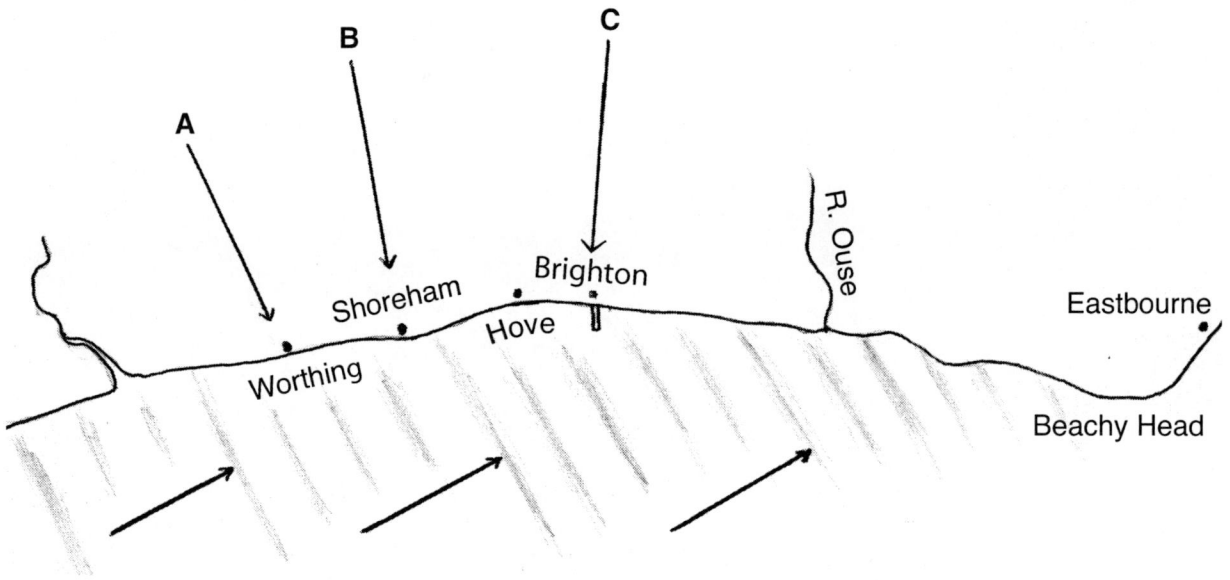

D Imagine you were part of the South Downs Shoreline Management Team with responsibility for sea defences along this stretch of coast. Looking at the case study above, what problems would you face? Which problems should be tackled first, and are there any long term solutions?

OR

Imagine you are writing a report for a local newspaper about the problems of coastal erosion. Chose one of the places above (A, B or C) and try to explain the problems and what is being done to solve them.

Chapter Four

Coastal Deposition

In the last chapter we saw how longshore drift removes beach material from the shore. When this **erosion** takes place it is **transported** (a process known as **transportation**) and then **deposited** further along the coast. So while sand and shingle is removed from one place, fresh land is created somewhere else. Where, and in what shape or form this land takes, will depend on the geography of the coastline, but typically the following features may be formed:

Spits

Spits are tongues of beach material created by longshore drift where there is a change in the direction of the coast, such as at a river mouth. Sand may build up as low ridges, to be added to and grow, or be a temporary feature that could be swept away by the next storm. The waves can cause the spit to curl around at the end. A shallow area of calm water called a **lagoon** can be created behind the spit. This may become a **salt marsh**, or could dry up to form new land. An example of a spit can be found at Spurn Head, at the mouth of the Humber Estuary.

Figure 1

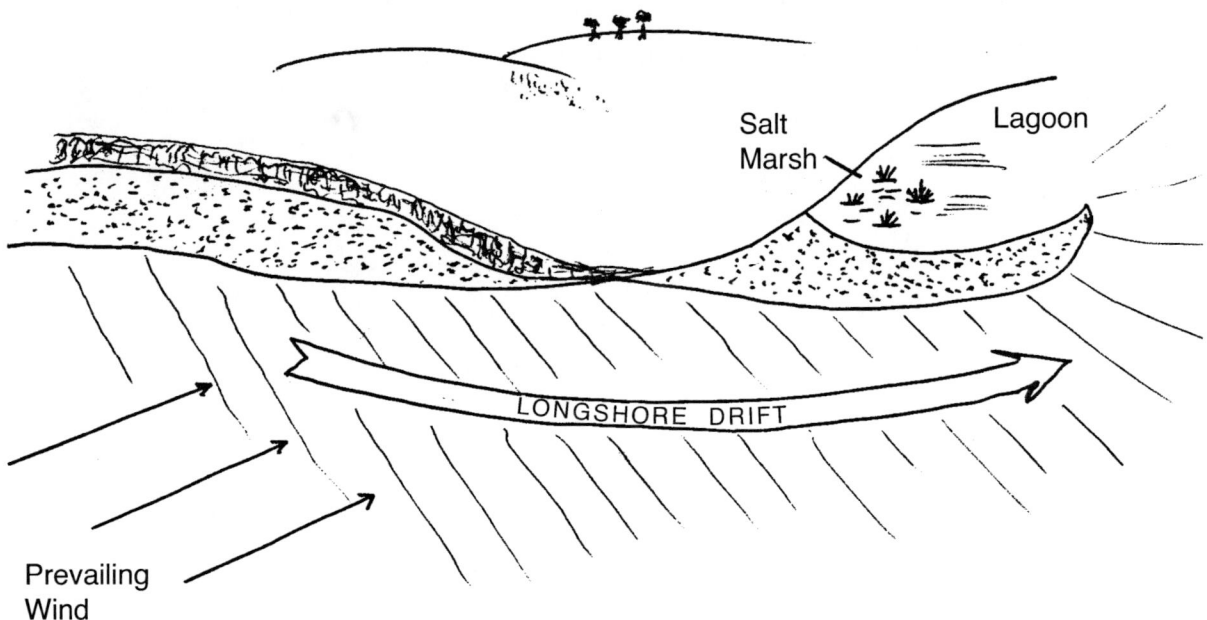

Bars

Similar to spits, these are low sand banks that form off-shore and often run parallel to the coast. Bars are formed whenever one moving body of water meets another, such as a river meeting the sea (or a lake, or another river). Again, their growth will depend on local conditions, such as the depth of the sea bed, perhaps the presence of a river mouth, as well as longshore drift. They can create barrier islands, protecting the coastal swamps nearer the shore. Examples can be seen at Chesil Beach in Dorset (see the Case study below) or more extensive ones at Cape Hatteras, North Carolina, U.S.A.

Figure 2

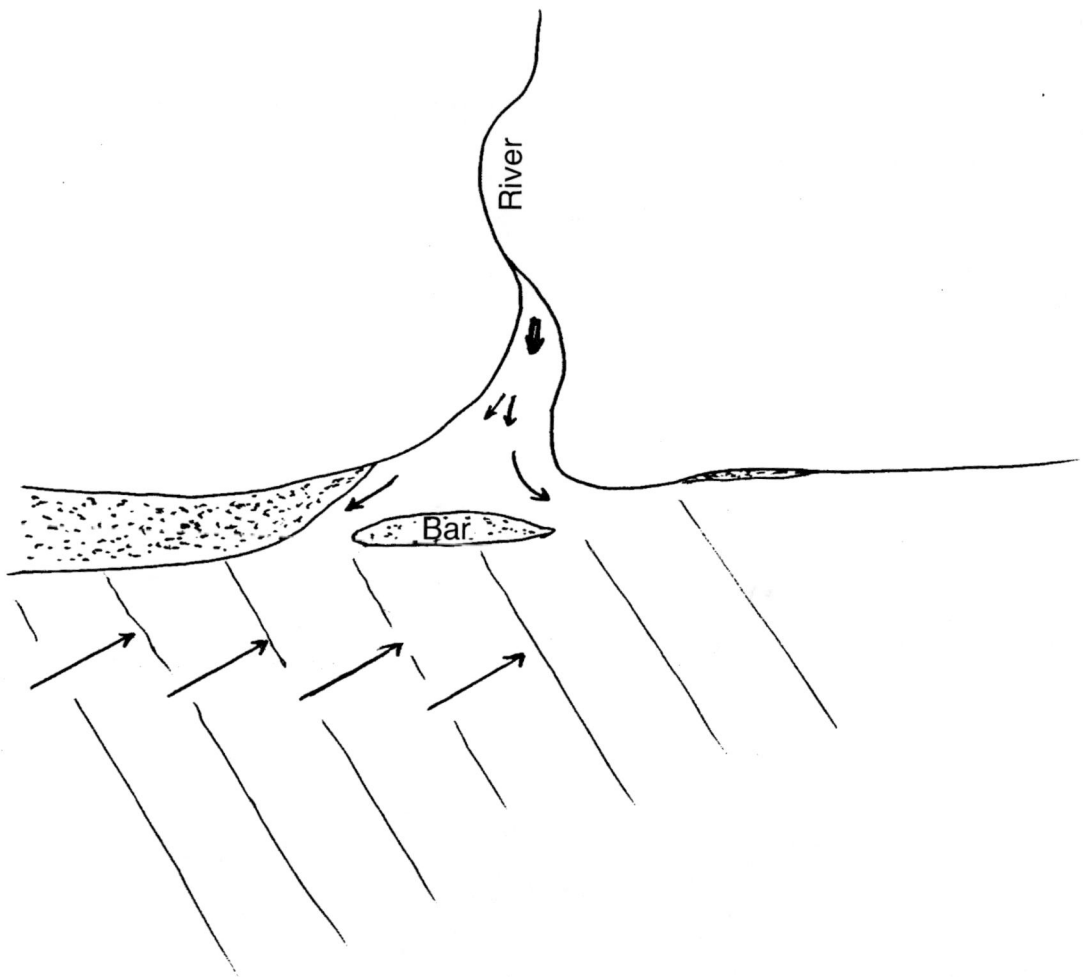

Tombolos

Sometimes there may be an island a little way offshore. If longshore drift occurs along the mainland the island may become attached to the shore as sand builds up, making a natural causeway. This new feature is given the Italian name, tombolo. An example of a tombolo is Portland Bill in Dorset.

Figure 3

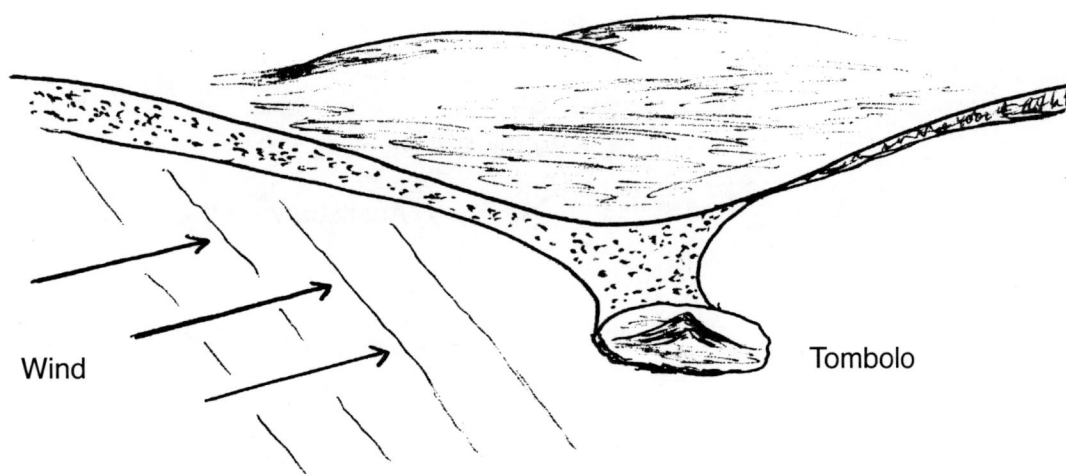

Wind

Tombolo

Case Study:
The Jurassic Coast, Chesil Beach, and Portland Bill, Dorset

In 1811 Mary Anning found the skeleton of an ichthyosaurus near Lyme Regis. Her discovery started off the search for fossils preserved in the limestone that continues to the present day. Now known as the Jurassic Coast, it runs 150 km from Exmouth in east Devon to Studland Bay in Dorset and is designated a World Heritage Site. The cliffs regularly give up fossils of ammonites and other sea creatures that lived 100 to 320 million years ago.

Figure 4

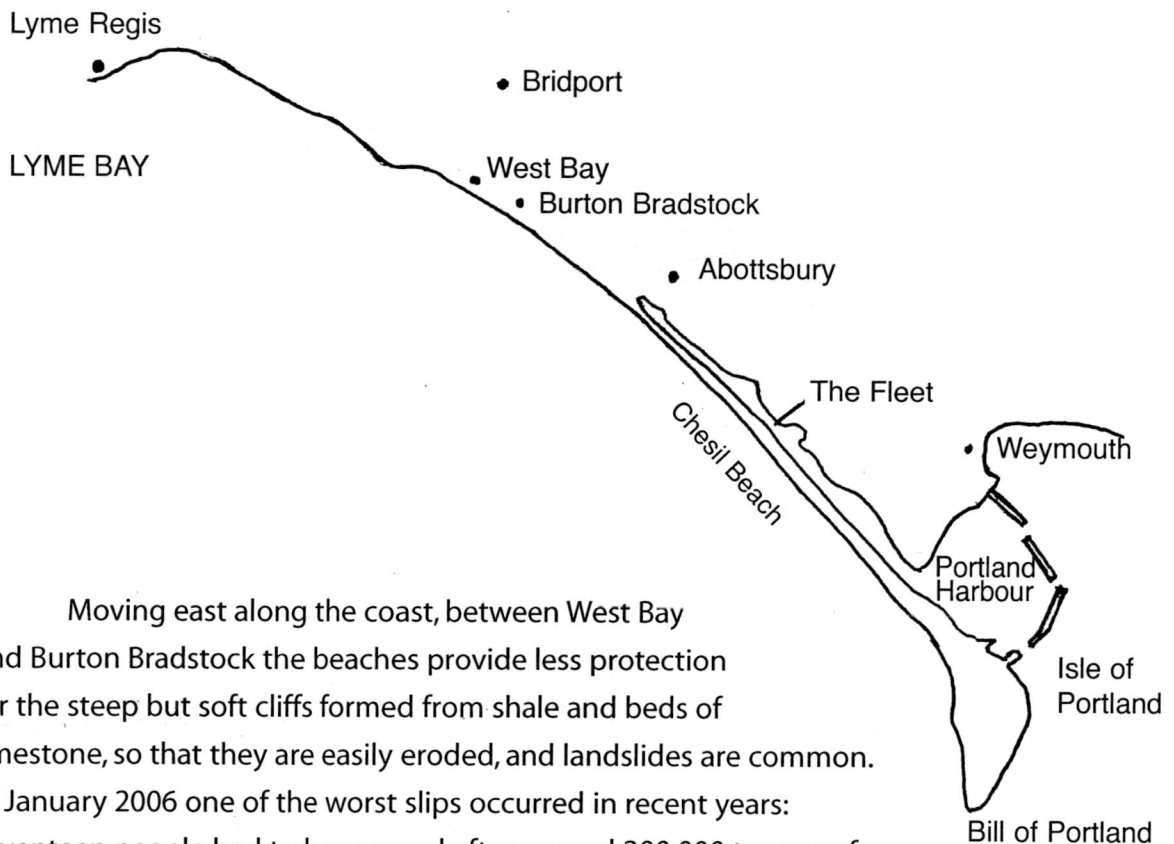

Moving east along the coast, between West Bay and Burton Bradstock the beaches provide less protection for the steep but soft cliffs formed from shale and beds of limestone, so that they are easily eroded, and landslides are common. In January 2006 one of the worst slips occurred in recent years: seventeen people had to be rescued after around 200,000 tonnes of earth and mud collapsed onto the beach. It created a fresh bonanza for fossil hunters, although the beach was closed for some time after to protect the public from further slips. Some 22 million people, many being fossil hunters, visit the Jurassic Coast each year.

In some places the land has slipped only so far, stopping partly between the top of the cliff and the beach. Porous rock is sandwiched between layers of impervious clays and shales that tilt towards the beach. In time, rainwater collects and increases the weight of the porous layer until the whole section becomes unstable and slips. This `undercliff` forms an open habitat, naturally protected from man, that has become colonised by plants and even full-grown trees, leading to a natural biodiversity.

Figure 5

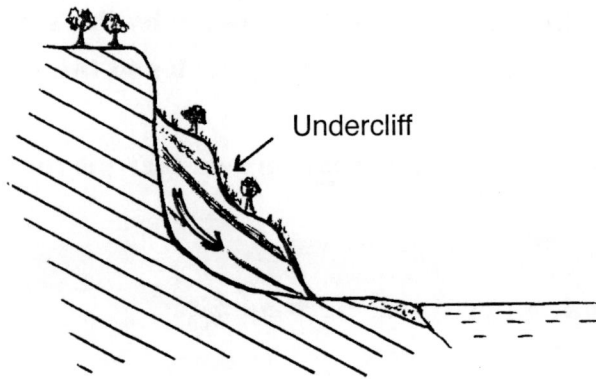

Chesil Beach extends for some 28 kms from West Bay to the `Isle` of Portland. It is made up of shingle, pebbles and large cobbles that have built up for over 7,000 years. The beach material has been graded by the sea so that pebbles get larger towards the east. The gradient of the beach also increases from west to east.

For 13 kms Chesil Beach protects the shallow tidal Fleet Lagoon that has been formed behind it. This is an important wildlife habitat, particularly for migrating sea birds. At Abbotsbury there is a swannery, once run by the Benedictine monks of the nearby monastery. Now a tourist attraction, during the breeding season the swans build over one hundred nests on or near the shore.

The eastern end of Chesil Beach forms a tombolo linking the Isle of Portland to the mainland. Behind it, and sheltered from the prevailing winds, is Portland Harbour, the naval base and the town of Chiswell. The peninsula of Portland has been scarred by quarrying, the famous light-brown stone being used for numerous buildings, including St Paul's Cathedral, as well as being ground up to produce Portland cement.

39

1. What sort of materials form Chesil Beach?

2. Try to explain how the beach material is sorted by the sea, so that smaller pebbles are found in the west, and large pebbles in the east.

3. The beaches along this stretch of coast are dangerous for swimming. Suggest why this is.

4. Try to find out about other World Heritage Sites.

5. Find out more about the type of fossils that can be found along the Jurassic Coast. What do they tell us about the climate when the creatures were living here?

6 Links with History:
   (a) Find out why many monasteries, such as the one at Abbotsbury, no longer exist.
   (b) Try to discover what use was made of Fleet Lagoon during World War Two.

7. Look at the diagram in Figure 6 (page 41). Considering the direction of the prevailing wind, mark on the diagram any features you think may be formed by longshore drift.

Figure 6

Coastal Deposition Simulation

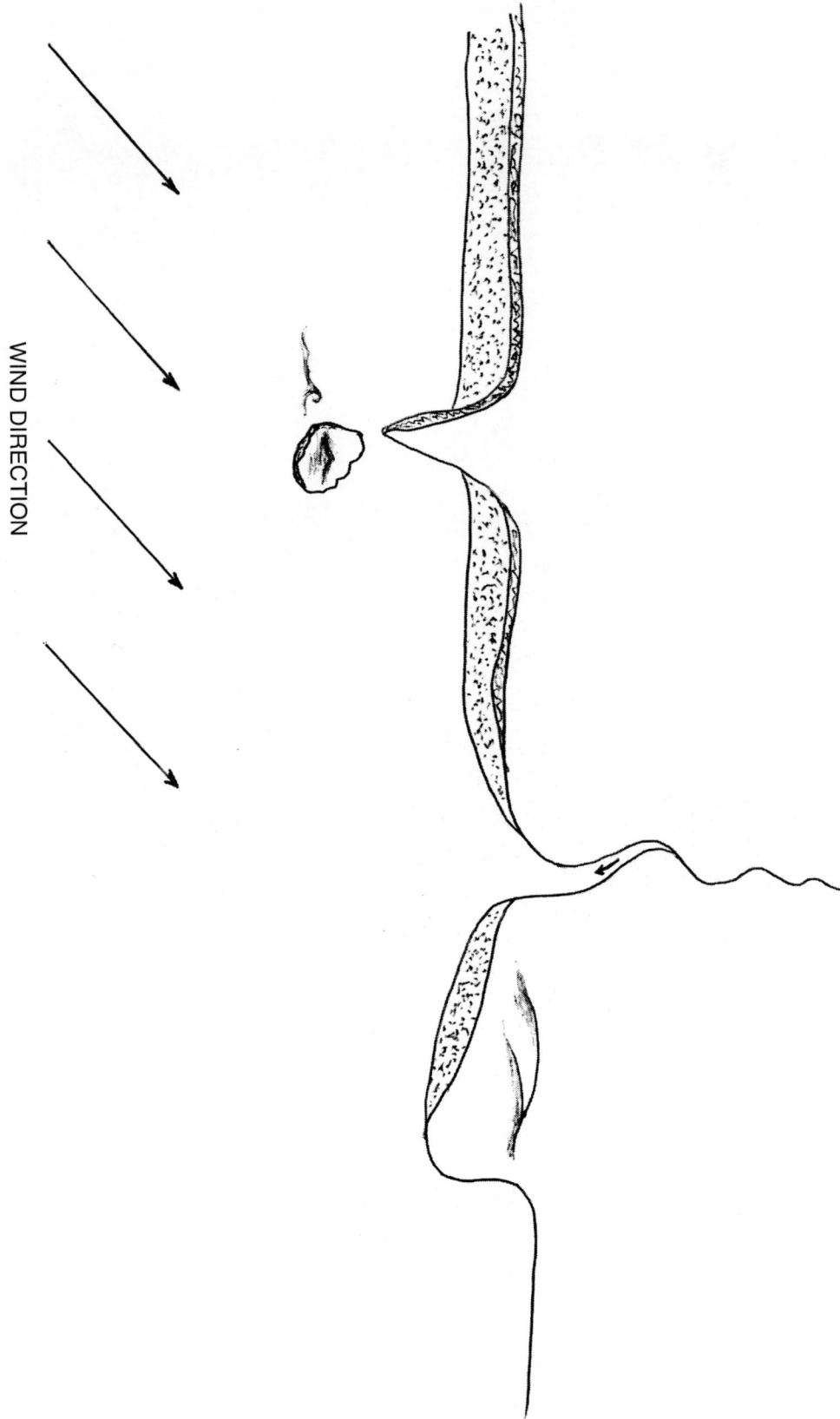

WIND DIRECTION

Chapter Five

Types of Coastline

Some parts of the British Isles are protected by tall **cliffs**, while at other places extensive areas of **sand dunes** are the only things to counter the force of the sea - see map, Figure 1 (page 46). Clearly, cliffs are permanent natural barriers, but sand dunes can be moved by the wind, and may grow or decrease in size.

Figure 2 - Dunes Moving

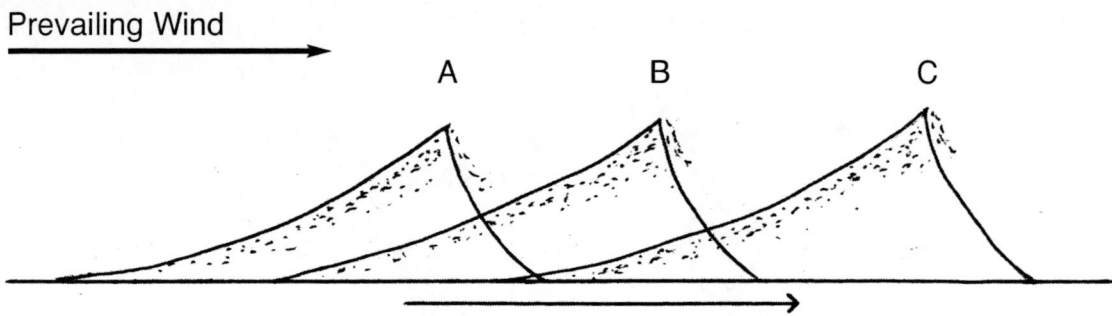

Case Study - St Piran's Church, Cornwall

The old St Piran's Church at Perranzabuloe in Cornwall was built in about 1150, replacing an older sixth-century oratory which had been buried in the sand. However, the same thing began to happen to this church, so that by 1793 sand had to be shovelled away before the church could be used for Sunday worship. In 1805 it was decided to give up the fight, and a new St Piran's Church was built some three kilometres away using much of the original building materials, including most of the tower which was dismantled stone-by-stone and transported to the new site.

Now, in 2006, the remains of the old church are being excavated from the sand by archaeologists, followed by conservation work to preserve it. Interpretation boards will be set up nearby to provide information about the church that was lost to the sand.

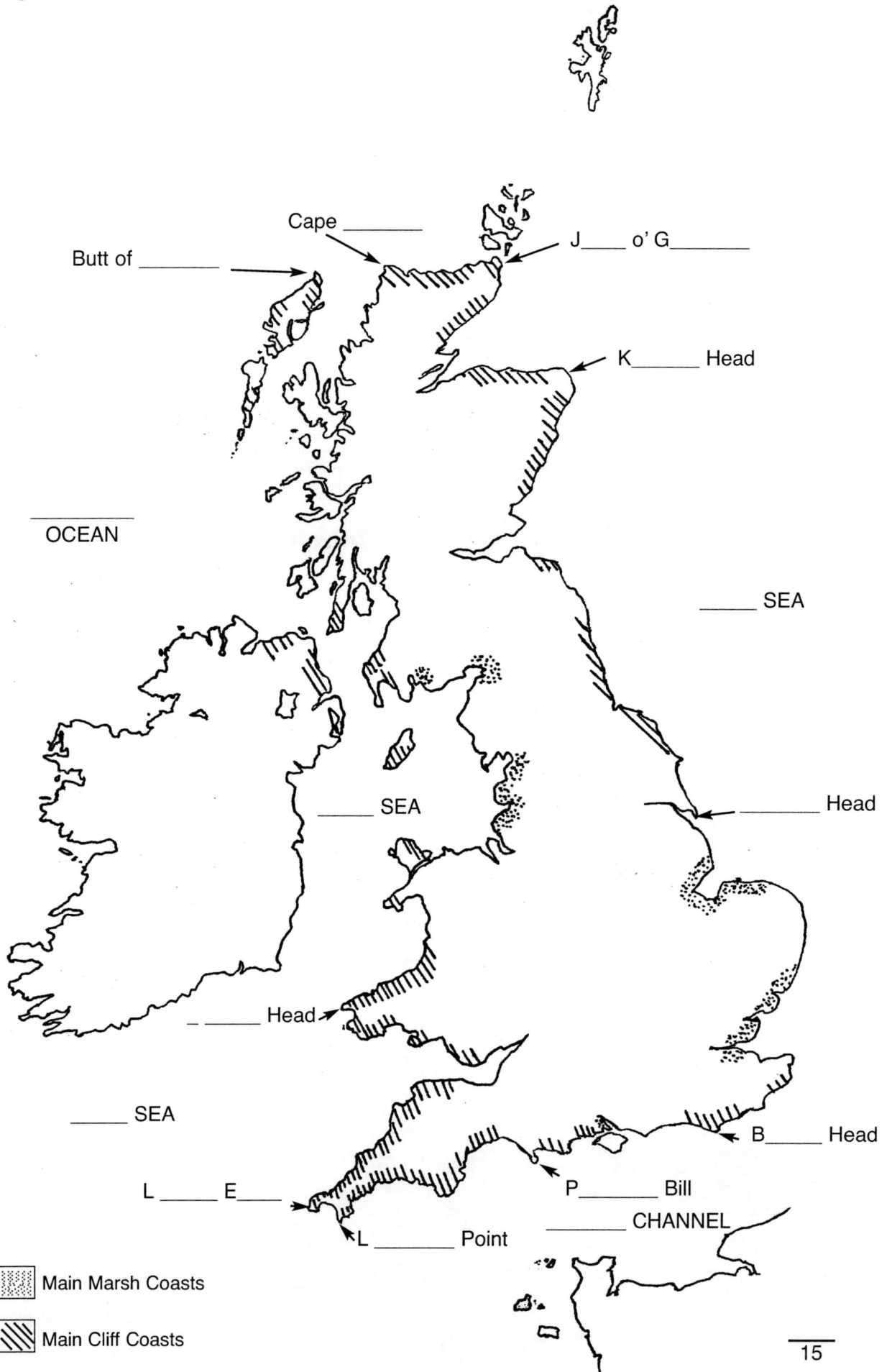

Figure 1

Cape _____

Butt of _____

J____ o' G_____

K_____ Head

_____ OCEAN

_____ SEA

_____ SEA

____ Head

SEA

_____ SEA

B_____ Head

L_____ E___

P_____ Bill

_____ CHANNEL

L_____ Point

Main Marsh Coasts

Main Cliff Coasts

15

46

Simulation Exercise: Stopping Dunes Moving

1. Using the diagram below, try to decide how you would stop the sand dunes moving and burying the church.

Figure 3

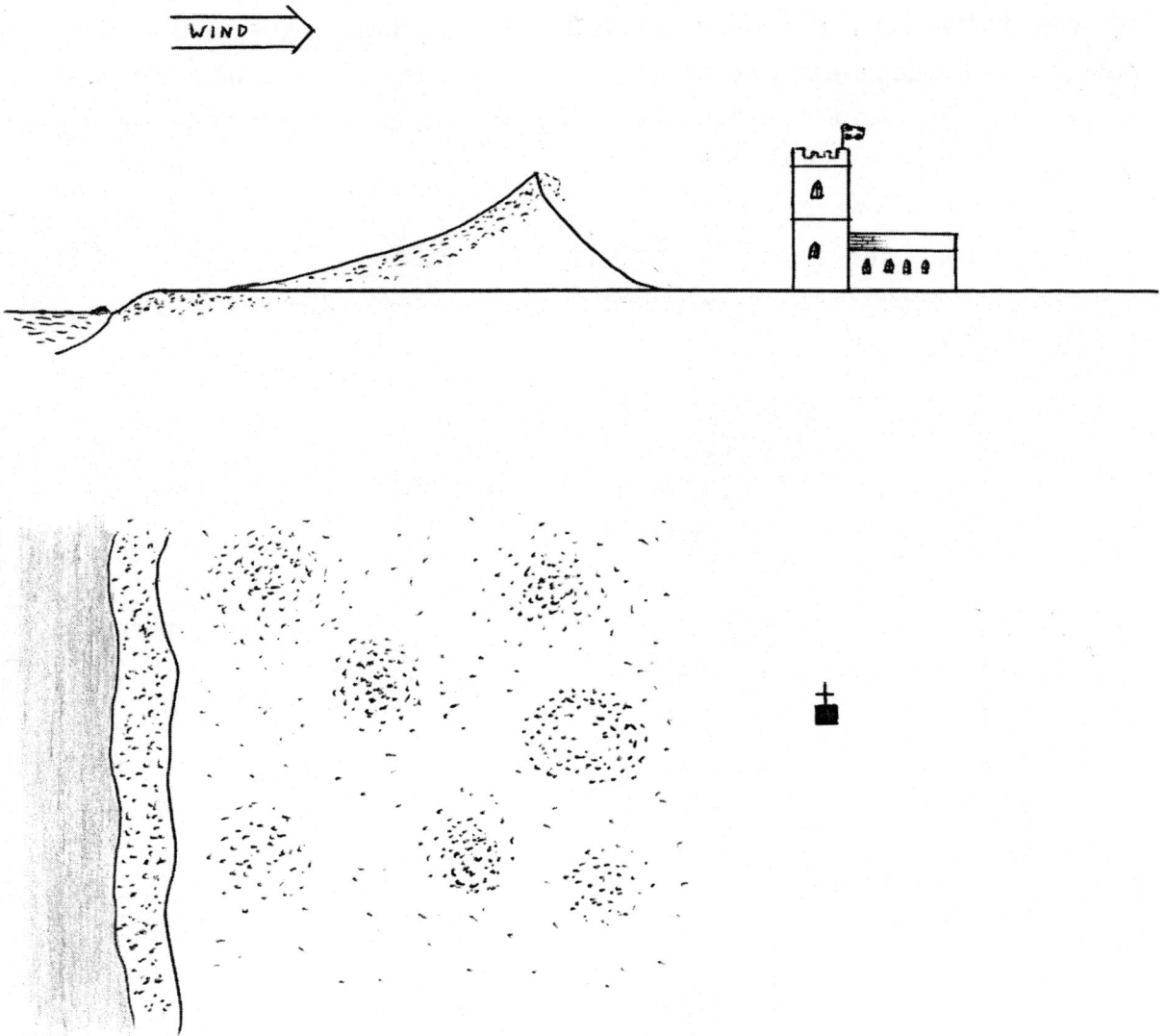

Stopping Dunes Moving

To stop sand dunes moving, marram grass is often planted. It has strong spiky leaves above the surface, while its extensive root system binds the loose sand together. Marram grass dislikes salt, so is not found near the high tide mark. As well as forming a natural barrier to the sea, such areas are often given over to nature reserves or turned into caravan parks or golf courses.

Salt marshes may be found in shallow lagoons behind spits or beside our many river mouths or estuaries. They are a natural meeting point of fresh river water and tidal salt water. Salt marsh plants have adapted to thrive in these conditions. Sometimes these areas can dry up and form fresh land as they are colonised by trees.

Mud Flats contain large quantities of decaying plant and animal matter, as well as particles of silt and clay. This means that just below the surface little oxygen is present, and bubbles of sulphide gases, giving the tell-tale smell of rotten eggs, may be experienced. However, they may support large numbers of edible clams and other creatures that have adapted to this environment.

Islands are areas of land surrounded by water. These can range in size from tiny islets to the largest island in the world, Greenland. Figure 4 shows some of major islands and island groups of the British Isles.

2. **Try to find out what it is like to live on one of these islands. What are the advantages and disadvantages of island life?**

3. **Look at Figure 1. Make up a table and sort out the following regions into two categories, sea cliffs or coastal marshes. You may find an atlas useful.**

The Wash	The Mull of Kintyre	Cardigan, Wales
Cornwall	The Isle of Man	Dover
Essex	Northumberland	North Devon
Morecambe Bay		

Figure 4

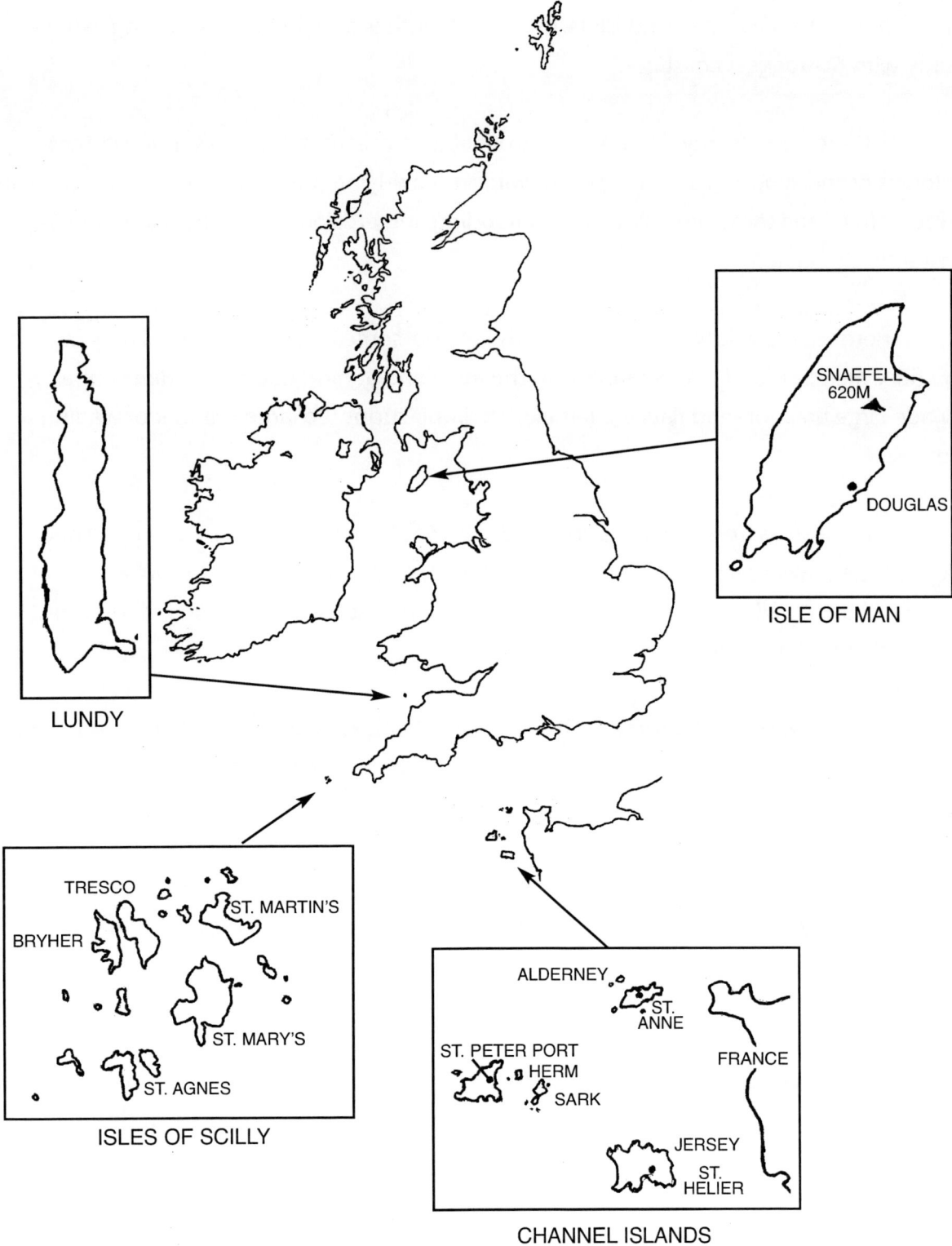

LUNDY

ISLE OF MAN

SNAEFELL
620M

DOUGLAS

ISLES OF SCILLY

TRESCO
BRYHER
ST. MARTIN'S
ST. MARY'S
ST. AGNES

CHANNEL ISLANDS

ALDERNEY
ST.
ANNE
ST. PETER PORT
HERM
FRANCE
SARK
JERSEY
ST.
HELIER

Not to scale

Case Study: The Essex Marshes

These are found in an area running from the border of Greater London and the north coast of the River Thames, then north to Harwich and the River Stour. The direct distance along the coast may be only 80 kilometres but because the coastline changes direction so many times with many inlets and islets, its actual length is about 650 kms, making Essex the county with the longest coastline.

As there are so many different types of habitats this stretch of coast is important ecologically and supports a wide range of wildlife. Low-lying mud flats and salt marshes can be found here, and these are vulnerable to flooding and erosion, so that the landscape is constantly changing.

There are many low-lying islands in the region, some permanent, others only cut off at high tide. Mersea Island is separated from the mainland at high tide by a wide channel. At low tide large areas of mud flats are left exposed, and support a large number of wading birds.

In some areas freshwater grazing land is protected from the sea by a sea wall and dyke. On the seaward-side salt marsh may be found, such as at Salcott. Here a freshwater drainage channel called a Borrowdyke was created when soil was `borrowed` during the construction of the sea wall.

Until July 2000 the Ministry of Defence used Rainham Marshes as a firing range. This had the benefit of preserving this ancient landscape, so that when the RSPB acquired the area they became the custodians of the largest remaining stretch of wetland still bordering the upper reaches of the Thames Estuary. The reserve, of 350 hectares, forms 77% of the `Inner Thames Marshes Site of Special Scientific Interest`, and supports a great variety of wading birds as well as wildfowl, finches and even birds of prey, and is also a significant site for water voles.

Human use includes fisheries and farming. Tourism is also important with the estuaries and creeks being ideal for water sports such as yachting, while the resorts of Southend, Clacton-on-Sea, Frinton-on-Sea and Walton-on-the-Naze are popular destinations for people seeking seaside holidays.

Figure 5 - The Essex Marshes

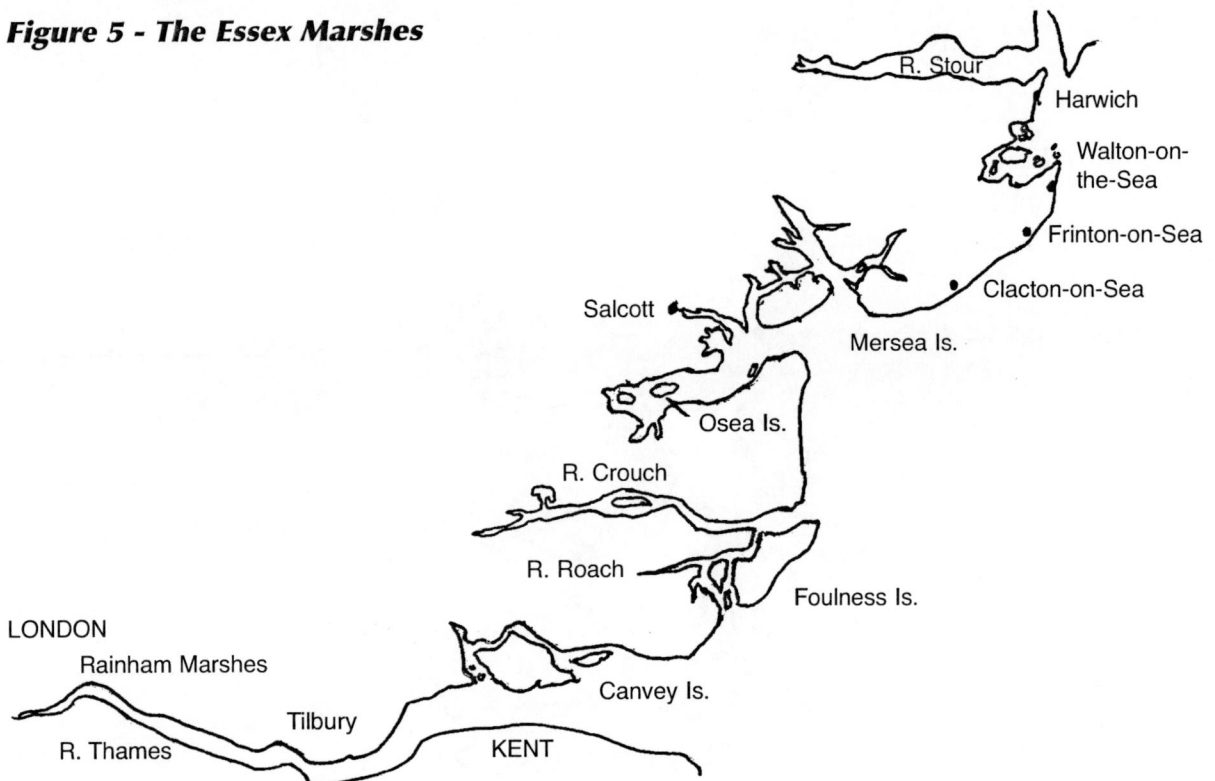

The Dartford Tunnel, first opened in 1963, and a second tunnel opened in 1980, as well as Queen Elizabeth Bridge, cross the River Thames allowing people south of the river to reach Essex without travelling through central London.

4. Try to find out how much further the journey from Dartford to Brentwood would be if these crossing points were not used.

5. Choose one of these crossings and try to find out about:

   (a) Their construction

   (b) The cost of maintaining them.

   (c) Looking at a map of the area and the position of settlements and roads, is there a need for another road link, and if so where? What other factors would need to be considered?

6. Use Figure 6 and an atlas to identify the major islands and inlets of the British Isles. (You may like to see how many you can identify before turning to the atlas.)

Islands

1 _____

2 _____

3 _____

4 _____

5 _____

6 _____

7 _____

8 _____

Inlets

9 _____

10 _____

11 _____

12 _____

13 _____

14 _____

15 _____

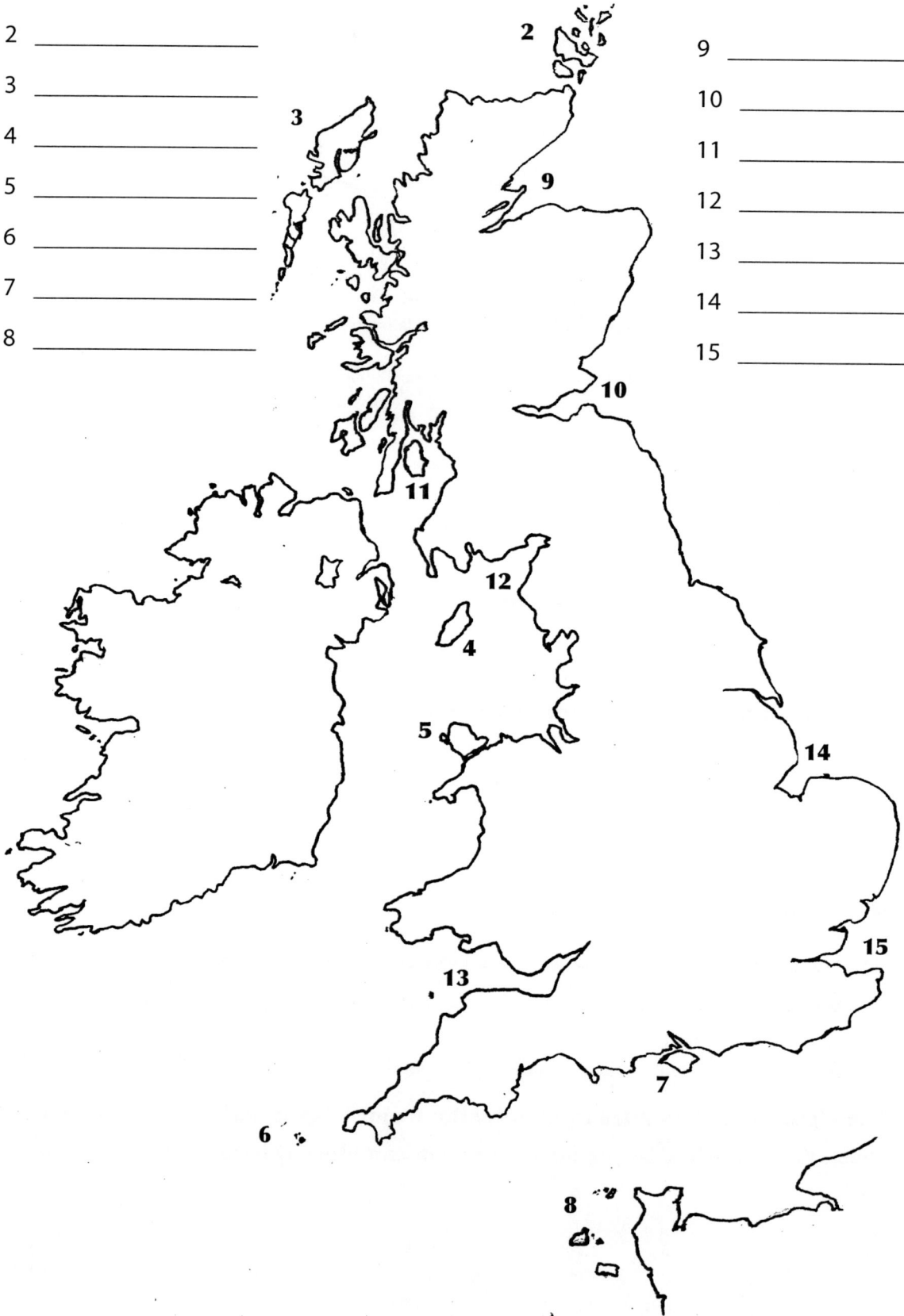

Chapter Six

Changing Sea Levels

Today we hear a great deal about global warming, climate change and the possible effects on sea levels. However, fluctuating sea levels are not new, we just happen to live during a relatively stable climatic period known as a post-glacial period. If sea levels do change, they will have an impact on our coasts, just as they did in the past.

The Earth has experienced several ice ages: the most recent began about 3 million years ago and ended about 11,000 years ago. During this time the sea level was lower as so much water was trapped on the land as ice, and northern Britain was covered by ice sheets. At the end of the ice age sea levels rose. Evidence for these changes can be seen today in drowned valleys. The variation was compounded by the fact that the land recovered somewhat once the weight of ice was gone, and the land forming the British Isles is tilting, with the eastern side sinking very slowly, while the west is rising.

As the sea level may rise or fall - and so can the land - so the meeting point of land and sea, our coasts, will be affected. This can create two types of coast, **submerged** and **emerged**.

Emerged Coasts

When there is a drop in sea level, a new shoreline is created. The old shore may be left suspended above the new one as a **raised beach**, leaving a tell-tale line of shingle and pebbles. Behind the raised beach there may be evidence of a **dead cliff**. The sea will no longer reach it, but it will still be affected by weathering.

Figure 1

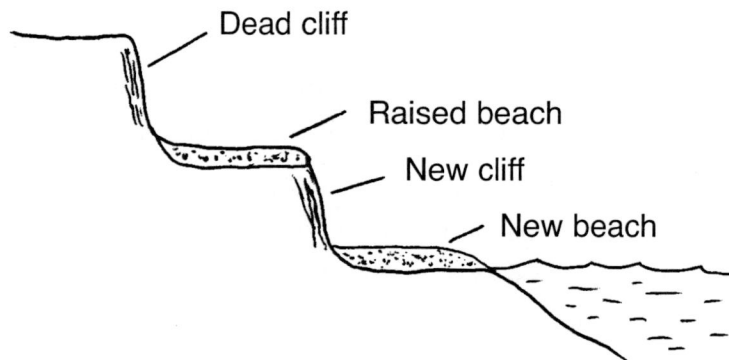

- Dead cliff
- Raised beach
- New cliff
- New beach

Submerged Coasts

As the sea level rises it may flood valleys leading to the sea. The flooded valleys are known as **rias** and may form part of a larger **ria coastline**. Where the land is less high they are often known as **estuaries**, for example the Thames Estuary or the Fal Estuary in the Case Study below.

If, rather than being at right angles to the sea, the hills and valleys run parallel to the shore, a **Dalmatian coast** may result. An example is Lulworth Cove in Dorset, while the Adriatic coast of Croatia provides a more extensive example with many long, thin islands left parallel with today's mainland.

Figure 2

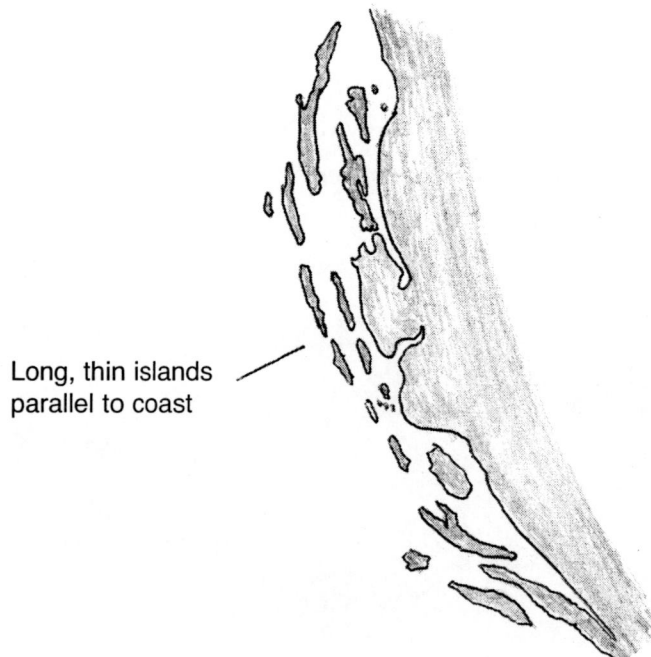

Long, thin islands parallel to coast

Valleys may have been deepened, widened and straightened by glaciers to create U-shaped valleys. If they were flooded by the sea at the end of the ice age steep-sided and deep **fjords** (or **fiords**) were left. These are often used as sheltered anchorages. Examples include the sea lochs of western Scotland and the west coast of Norway.

Figure 3

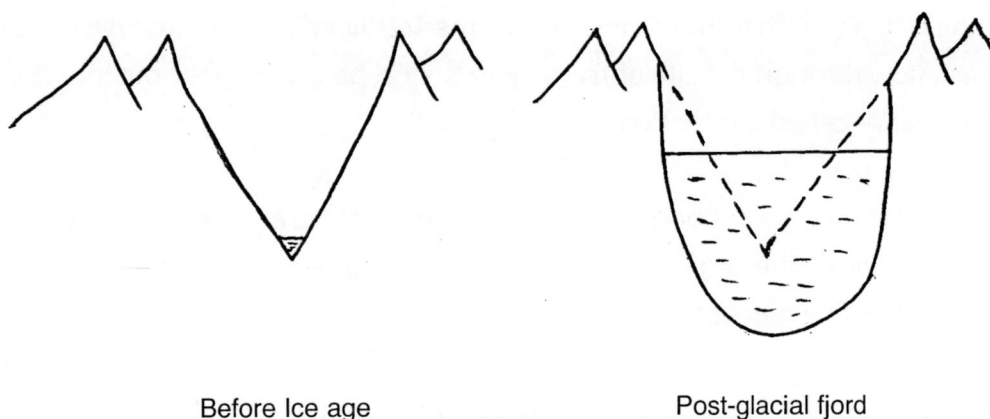

Before Ice age   Post-glacial fjord

Coral polyps are small creatures that extract calcium carbonate from sea water then secrete it to form hard external skeletons that build up into limestone **coral reefs.** These form various patterns, such as horseshoe-shaped atolls or fringing reefs that can build up offshore. The world's largest coral reef is the Great Barrier Reef off Queensland, Australia, which is about 2,200 kilometres in length.

Coral polyps only grow at certain sea temperatures (20° - 30° C) and at depths of no more than 50 metres, and also need clear water for they are dependent on sunlight. They are therefore at risk from global warming, pollution and rapidly rising sea levels.

Recent research in the Caribbean has shown that increases in sea temperature are already harming these microscopic algae, causing the coral to lose its colour or `bleach`. If sea temperatures continue to rise they could be killed, leaving large areas of dead reef. This would have an effect on the whole **ecosystem**, for the coral reefs are home to a wide variety of marine life, as well as being popular with divers and tourists. To get a clearer general picture of the bleaching or loss of colour, scientists are monitoring reefs around the world with satellites.

Case Study - The Fal Estuary, Cornwall

The source of the River Fal is on high land in the heart of the Cornish peninsula. During Roman times the river was navigable as far inland as the village of Tregony, but eventually it silted up with waste from local extraction industries such as tin and copper mines, and the china clay pits near St. Austell. (The world-famous Eden Project is located in a former china clay pit). Other tributaries, such as the Tresillian River and the rivers Truro and Allen - which flow through the city of Truro - join the Fal before it opens out into the junction of several estuaries called Carrick Roads (see Figure 4).

The estuary or ria was flooded at the end of the last ice age to create a wide and deep natural harbour, one of the largest in the world. Figure 5 gives an indication of what the area would have looked like before that time.

Taking advantage of its situation, the port of Falmouth gradually overshadowed the nearby town of Penryn to become the largest trading port in the Duchy by the eighteenth-century. Being in the southern-most part of Britain, merchant ships were replenished there before making long sailing voyages. For many years it was also the destination of packet ships bringing post and messages to the Royal Mail Packet Station in the town.

During the reign of Henry VIII castles were built at St. Mawes and the high Pendennis Point to protect the entrance to the estuary from possible attacks by the French. These were re-armed during World War II, when the town and nearby creeks provided a number of embarkation points for the D-Day landings in June 1944.

Today Falmouth Docks provides valuable facilities for ship repairing and refurbishment, as well as handling some bulk cargoes and a small but growing number of cruise ships. Falmouth and the many rivers and creeks provide sheltered moorings for yachtsmen. It is also an important resort for holidaymakers enjoying the unspoilt countryside and beaches.

1. **Add to Figure 4:**
   (a) A compass
   (b) Arrows to show the direction the rivers flow.
   (c) Label the English Channel.
   (d) Suggestions for sheltered yacht moorings.

2. **Write clear definitions for the following words from the case study:**

Source	Merchant ships
Peninsula	Packet ships
Chandler	Tributary
Embarkation	Creek
Replenish	Navigable

3. **In what ways may the Fal Estuary be a help and a hindrance to transport links between the west and east of the region?**

4. **Using diagrams and notes, explain how an estuary or ria may be formed.**

Links with History:

5. **Try to find out how the Germans made good use of the captured Norwegian fjords during the Second World War.**

Figure 4

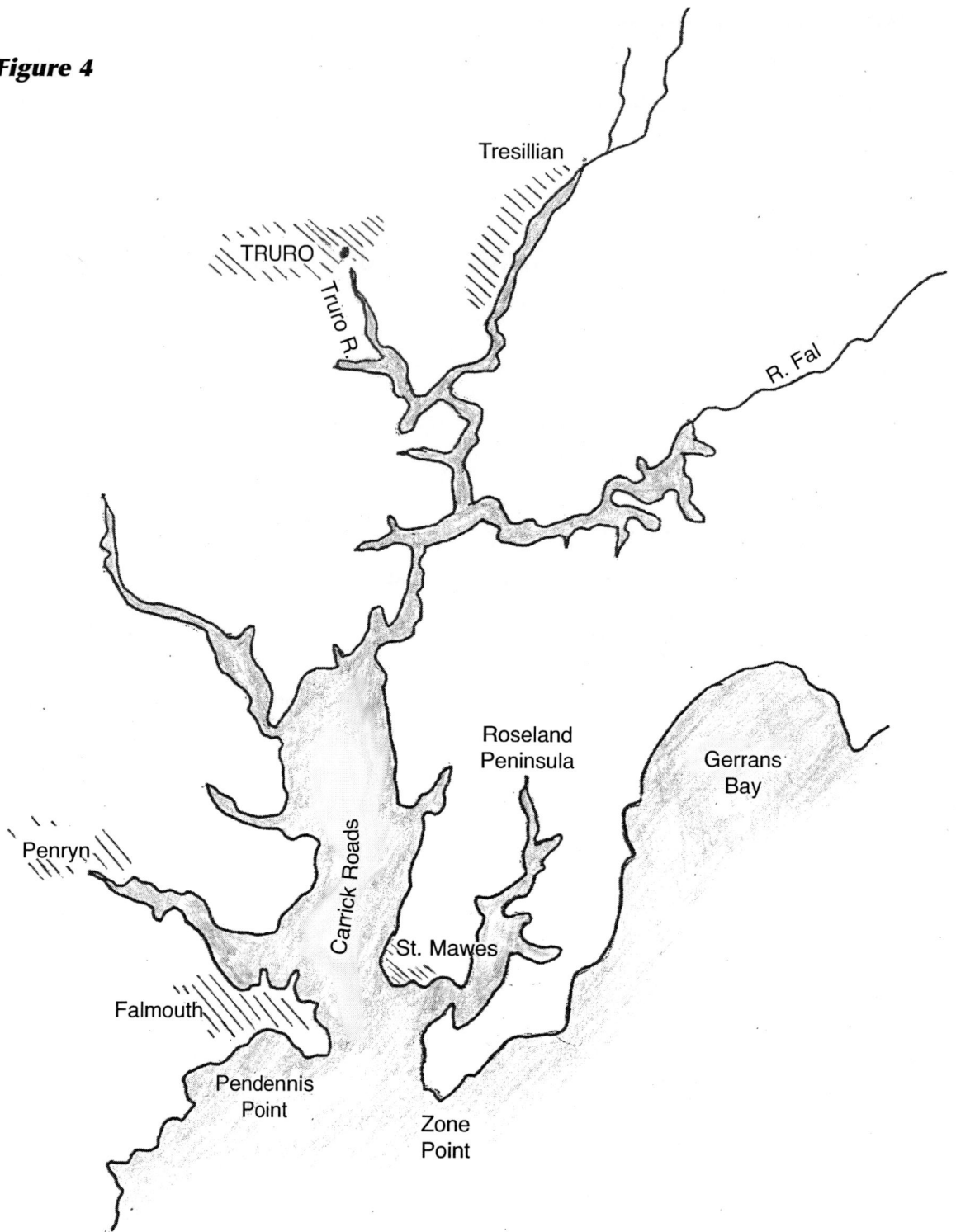

Tresillian

TRURO

Truro R.

R. Fal

Roseland
Peninsula

Gerrans
Bay

Penryn

Carrick Roads

St. Mawes

Falmouth

Pendennis
Point

Zone
Point

Figure 5

Present Sea Level

61

Chapter Seven

Coastal Flooding

As was seen in the last chapter, sea levels are likely to rise in coming years. This will have a dramatic effect on low-lying areas that may already be in danger of flooding during storms or high tides. In this chapter we will look at dramatic floods that have occurred within living memory, and an area that is at risk if sea levels continue to rise as predicted.

Causes of Coastal Flooding

*   High spring tides

*   Storm surges

*   Rising sea levels

*   Lack of drainage in low-lying areas

*   Climate change

*   Tsunami

The Effect of Rising Sea Levels

If current predictions come true, incidents of coastal flooding will increase in the coming decades. Global warming could result in large areas of polar regions melting. Large icebergs could break off from ice-sheets and drift further north or south, posing an increased danger to shipping: the North Atlantic shipping lanes between the USA/Canada and western Europe are the busiest in the world. It is possible that sea levels could rise by twenty metres in the next hundred years. Obviously low-lying areas such as Morecambe Bay, the Humber lowlands, the Somerset Levels, the Thames Estuary and much of south-east England would be at risk.

P
S
1. It is an interesting exercise to draw a map of Britain, western Europe or the world and show the shape of the land if the sea level was to rise by a significant amount. (The height chosen for your map will depend on the scale used in your atlas.)

Case Study 1 - Past Disaster: The 1953 East Coast Floods

On 31 January 1953 Britain's worst floods (and worst natural disaster) to date occurred after sea levels rose by more than two metres above the normal high water mark. The east coast, from the River Humber to Kent, was badly affected.

Causes

A combination of factors caused this to happen. The weather at the time resulted from an area of low pressure (a depression) passing the north of Scotland and veering into the North Sea. This created a **storm surge**, when strong north winds drove a mass of water into the bottleneck created by the narrow Straits of Dover. This coincided with a high spring tide. Flood defences were inadequate, there was no flood warning system at the time, communications to organise an evacuation were poor, and the emergency services were ill-prepared.

Effects

The sea defences were breached and parts of East Anglia, Essex and Kent - a quarter of the land being below sea level - were inundated. At Canvey Island in Essex 160,000 hectares of land were submerged: one hundred people drowned and 13,000 were evacuated. It was a similar story at Great Yarmouth, Lowestoft and Clacton. In the latter 37 people drowned in the town and neighbouring villages. As far north as Mablethorpe 5,000 people needed to be evacuated from their homes. In all, 307 people lost their lives in the floods, over 30,000 were evacuated and 24,500 houses were damaged. Apart from the human tragedy, in today's figures it would cost about £5 billion to put right.

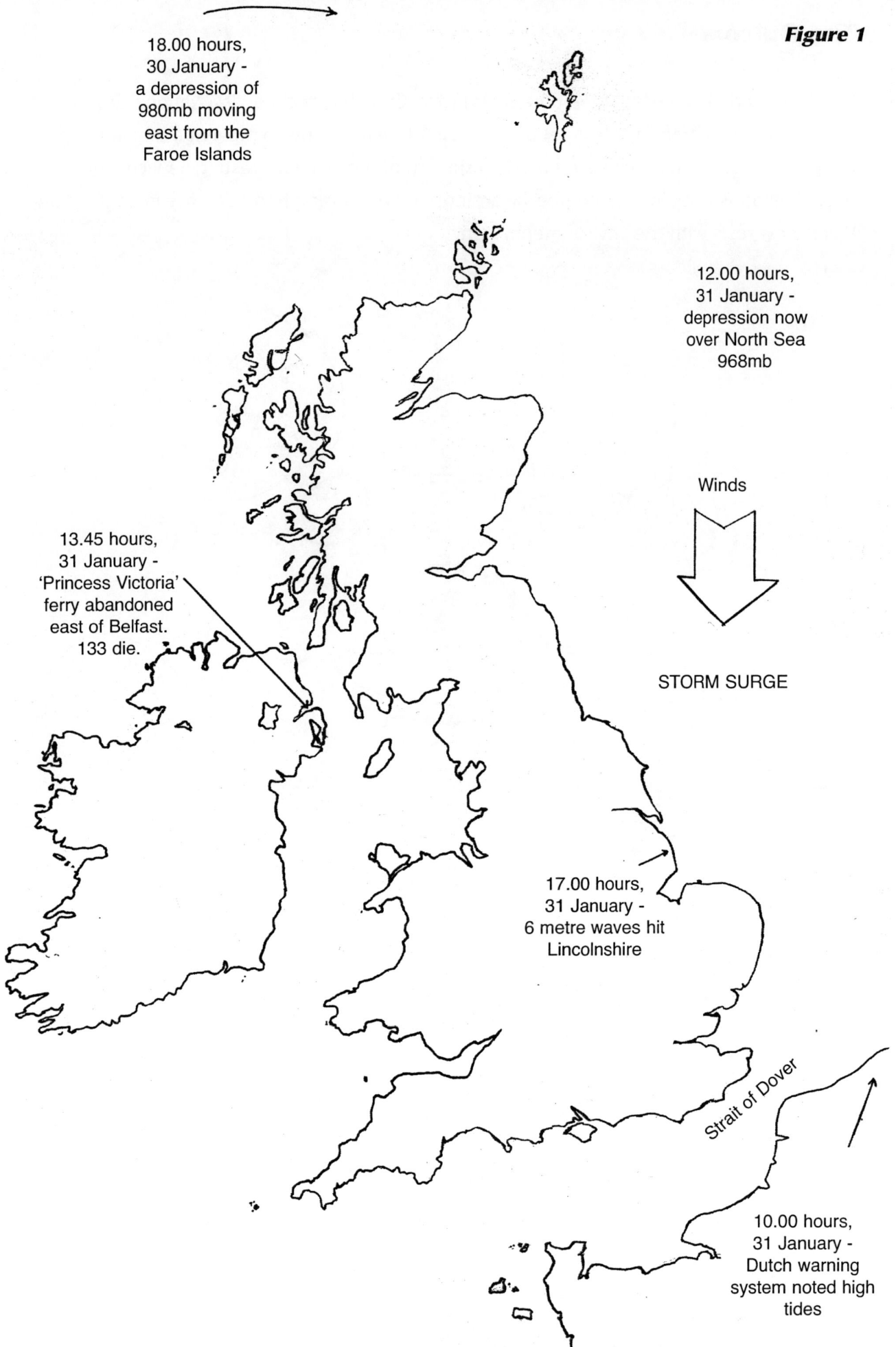

Figure 1

18.00 hours, 30 January - a depression of 980mb moving east from the Faroe Islands

12.00 hours, 31 January - depression now over North Sea 968mb

Winds

STORM SURGE

13.45 hours, 31 January - 'Princess Victoria' ferry abandoned east of Belfast. 133 die.

17.00 hours, 31 January - 6 metre waves hit Lincolnshire

Strait of Dover

10.00 hours, 31 January - Dutch warning system noted high tides

The Outcome

The Prime Minister at the time, Sir Winston Churchill, declared it a National Disaster. As a result of this a committee was set up to put in place measures to prevent a similar thing happening again. This included the establishment of the Tide Forecasting Service. The overall responsibility for issuing flood warnings and organising flood defence in England and Wales now rests with the Environment Agency.

If predictions prove correct, then flooding will become more frequent, particularly in low-lying areas near the coast, as in the following example:

Case Study 2 - Future Prospects: The Norfolk Broads

Large parts of the Norfolk Broads are below sea level, and are protected from the sea by beaches, flood defences, river management and efficient drainage. However, as sea levels rise, homes, farmland and natural habitats will be at risk. Now the Broadlands Flood Alleviation Project has been set up to improve the defences.

Surprisingly, the Broads are man-made features, the shallow lakes or `Broads` having been dug out for peat during the Middle Ages to provide fuel. These excavations flooded during the fourteenth-century when sea levels rose, creating a 200 km network of rivers and Broads. Traditionally, water levels were controlled by windmills operating pumps - during the nineteenth-century there were over 240 drainage mills in the Broads - but later electric pumps were employed. Peat is no longer dug here, but there has been a revival in reed-cutting for thatched roofs, and sailing and cruising remain popular with a large number of tourists who visit the Broads.

Of the forty Broads, the five major ones are Wroxham, Barton, Hickling, Ormesby and Filby. Hickling Broad, the largest and possibly the most well-known, is part of a nature reserve where a wide variety of bird life can be seen, including spoonbills during the summer. During the 1930s a number of coypus (nutrias) escaped from a Norfolk fur farm and remain at large in the area. These 60 cm-long aquatic rodents originating from South America are considered by many to be pests because of the damage they do to the native wildlife.

Coypus and rising sea levels are not the only threat to the ecology: the amount of salt (the salinity) in the water has been increasing. As more fresh water has been removed (or abstracted) for domestic or agricultural use, so there has been less available to counter high tides. At some point a decision may have to be made about the type of environment we want in the Broads. If sea levels rise too much it may mean that a freshwater habitat is no longer **sustainable**. Alternatively, it may be necessary to sustain just the area furthest from the sea and estuaries as fresh water Broads.

2. What influence has man had on this area?

3. Why might the environment of the Broads be unsustainable in the future?

4. We have seen how escaped coypus are considered a pest. Try to find out about coypu or other introduced species, such as grey squirrels, boar, or rats on Lundy, and the problems they cause and what, if anything, is being done about them.

5. How much should man interfere in the ecology of an area, or should it be left to nature to decide what the environment is like?

6. Compare the floods of 1953 with what could happen in the Norfolk Broads.

   Using a map of the area to help you, try to predict what could happen here, and what lessons could be learnt from the earlier tragedy. Think about the coastline where sea defences might be breached, low-lying areas, and settlements that may be at risk.

Chapter Eight

Coastal Defences

Coastal defences can be divided into two categories, **hard** and **soft** engineering. Hard engineering is when attempts are made to control the impact of the sea on our coasts with `hard` rigid man-made structures, such as the examples below. Soft engineering tries to work with nature, employing natural defences and using `soft` materials, such as sand.

Hard Engineering

Groynes

These are barriers made of wood or rock that run down a beach and extend into the sea. The movement of sand along the coast is slowed down, although it is often heaped up against the groynes in fan shapes. They are quite expensive to build and maintain. Near Felixstowe in Suffolk fishtail-shaped groynes have been built.

Concrete Walls

These are often used in relatively short lengths and to protect coastal towns and villages. They are expensive to build, and may still require groynes to be built to protect any beach in front of them.

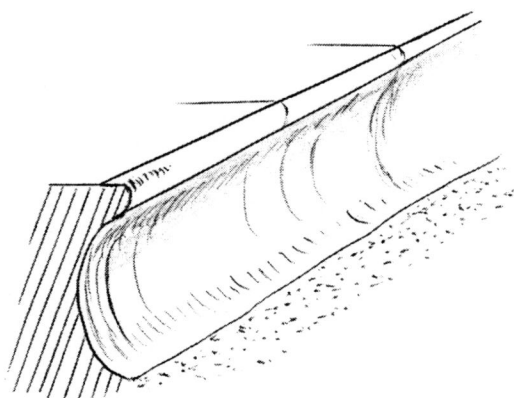

Revetments or Rock Armour

Large boulders can be positioned at the foot of cliffs to provide them with additional protection by breaking the force of the waves. However, they can look unsightly and intrusive. Near Felixstowe, Suffolk, rows of old barges have been sunk in the sand to break up the incoming tides.

Artificial Bays

These small sheltered coves can be created by piling up small islands of rock running parallel to the coast, which act like small breakwaters or reefs. They are expensive to set up, can be de-stabilized by powerful storms and can look unnatural. At Sea Palling in Norfolk a line of granite reefs has been built to protect the coast from erosion, as well as the Norfolk Broads further inland.

Soft Engineering

Drainage

Providing drainage at the top of cliffs can reduce the risk of their collapse.

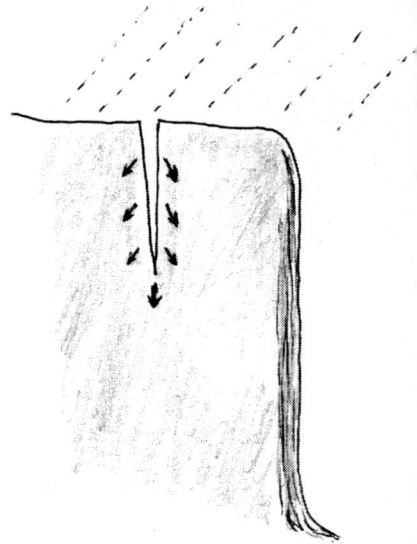

Beach-feeding

Sand can be replaced in areas where it has been lost because of storms or longshore drift, often by taking material that has built up to an excessive level elsewhere. However, it requires the movement of heavy machinery, and still may not last long.

Controlled flooding

There is an argument for allowing some low-lying areas to flood. It has been found that protecting one area of shore can lead to the problem moving further along the coast. Flooding of less important areas may act as a safety-valve, reducing the energy elsewhere and providing somewhere for excess water to go until it recedes naturally. The area can then be left as a salt marsh.

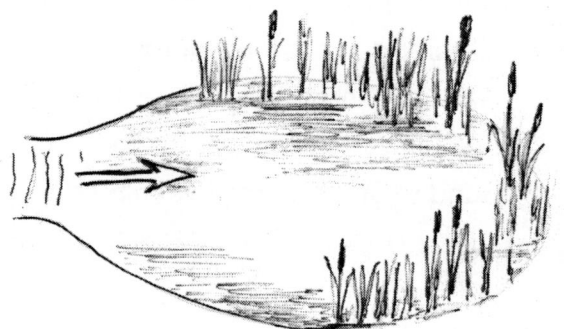

74

An Example of Coastal Defences

Figure 1 - Sea Wall at Seaton, South Devon(west of the Jurassic Coast)

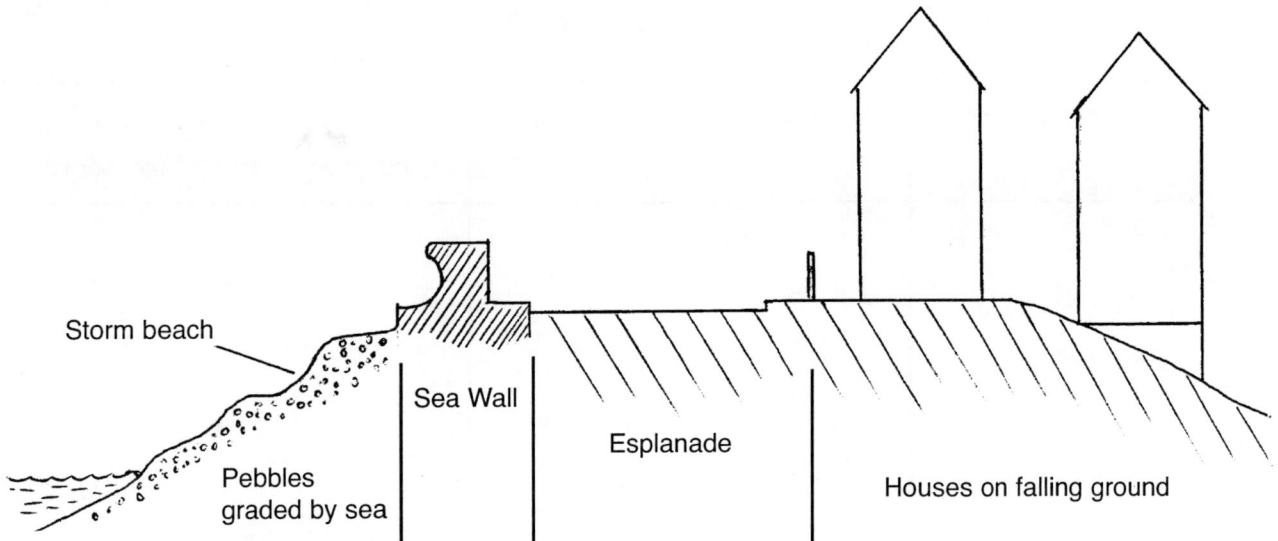

1. **Why do people continue to live close to the sea?**

2. **Who do you think should pay for coastal defences? (You could consider owners of coastal property, council tax payers, insurance companies, the government or European Union.)**

3. **Look at Figure 1.**
   (a) **What evidence is there that a sea wall is required here?**
   (b) **Why is the sea wall shaped like it is?**
   (c) **Why might the beach not be ideal for holiday-makers?**
   (d) **What would be the consequences if the sea wall was breached?**

4. **From what you have learnt, do you think all the coast of the British Isles should be protected in some form or other?**

5. **Try to find out how coastal defence is managed in the Netherlands.**

6. Using the information above, make up a table using the format below:

Sea Defences

Type of Defence	Advantages/Disadvantages	Environmental Impact (* equals bad to **** for good)

Case Study - The Thames Barrier

Following the east coast floods of 1953 (see Chapter 7) which claimed over 300 lives, it was clear that further flood defences would be needed to protect the heavily populated but low-lying capital. In 1974 work started on the Thames Barrier. It was completed in 1982 so that, along with the Barking Barrier, the Dartford Creek and Fobbing Horse Barriers, and gates at the entrances to the old Royal Docks, the upper Thames would be protected from excessive high tides or tidal surges. The problem for the designers was to create a barrier to retain the water, yet allow the passage of ships up and down the river (in a similar manner to Tower Bridge further upstream).

The Thames Barrier is formed by a line of ten movable gates running some 520 metres across the river and located on concrete pillars, like small islands, sunk into the bed of the river. When not in use six of them drop into recessed concrete cills in the riverbed so they don't hinder river traffic (see Figure 2). Inside each of the stainless steel-clad towers are two hydraulic rams that revolve the massive gates from a horizontal position on the river bed when not needed, to a vertical position to form a barrier, as well as revolving further so maintenance work can be carried out. The four main gates are hollow and constructed from steel plates. Each is over 20 metres high, and extend out from circular pivots. Together with their counterweights they weigh about 3,700 tonnes. They have been designed to hold back a load of over 9,000 tonnes.

Even this modern structure has a finite life span, and will need to be upgraded or replaced in the near future, especially if some forecasts of higher sea levels come true.

Figure 2 - Cross Section of the Thames Barrier

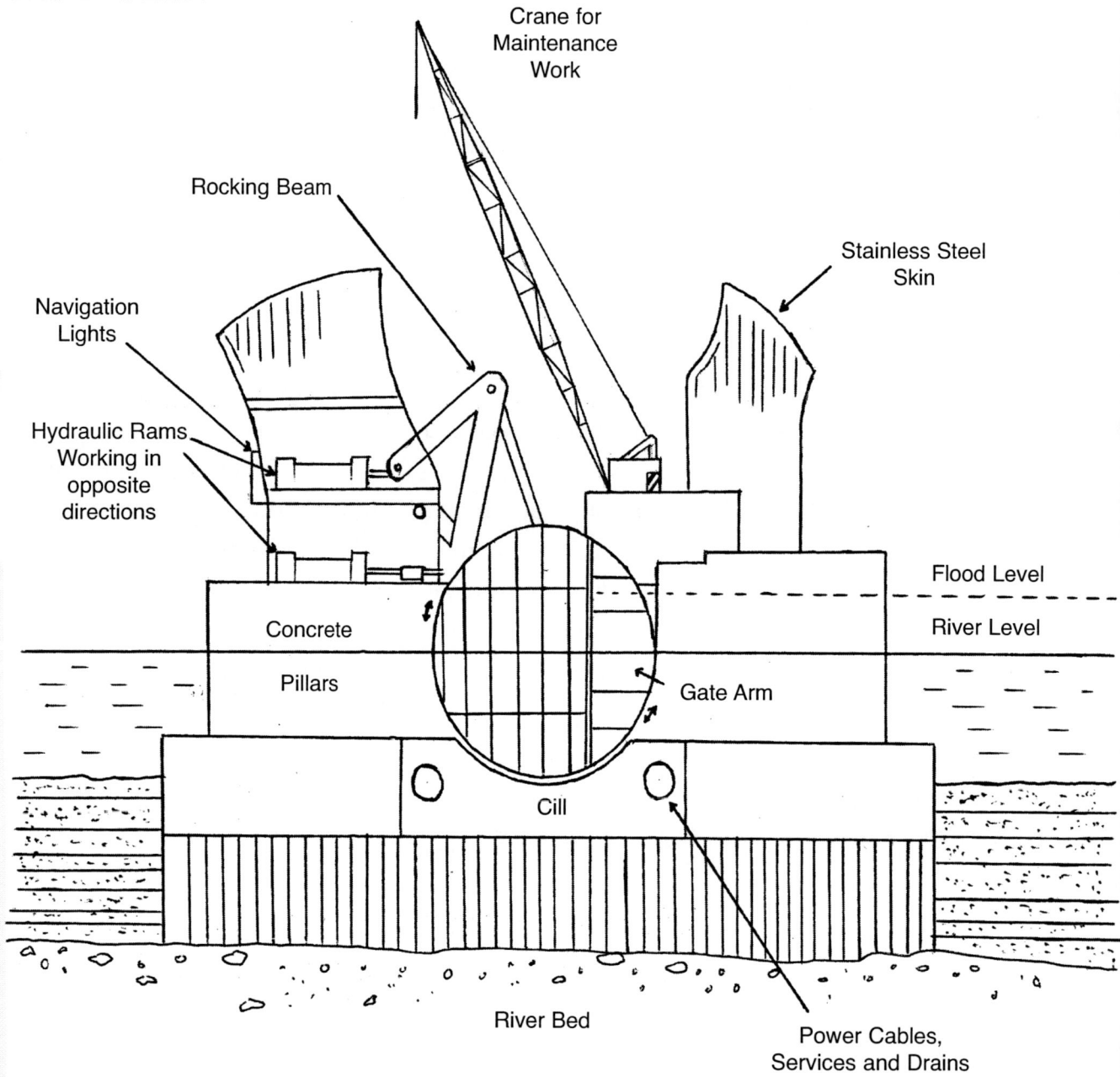

Figure 2 - Cross Section of the Thames Barrier

Crane for Maintenance Work

Rocking Beam

Stainless Steel Skin

Navigation Lights

Hydraulic Rams Working in opposite directions

Concrete

Pillars

Flood Level

River Level

Gate Arm

Cill

River Bed

Power Cables, Services and Drains

7. Using the information in the case study above, as well as Figure 2, explain how the Thames Barrier works.

8. Do you think the barrier will be used more or less frequently in future? Explain why.

S 9. How successful is the barrier?

D 10. Try to find out about other large cities, either in the UK or abroad, that could be at risk from rising sea levels.

11.

Simulation - Sea Defences

Mark on to the diagram below four types of sea defences you would use to protect this stretch of coast. You may like to add a suitable key.

Figure 3

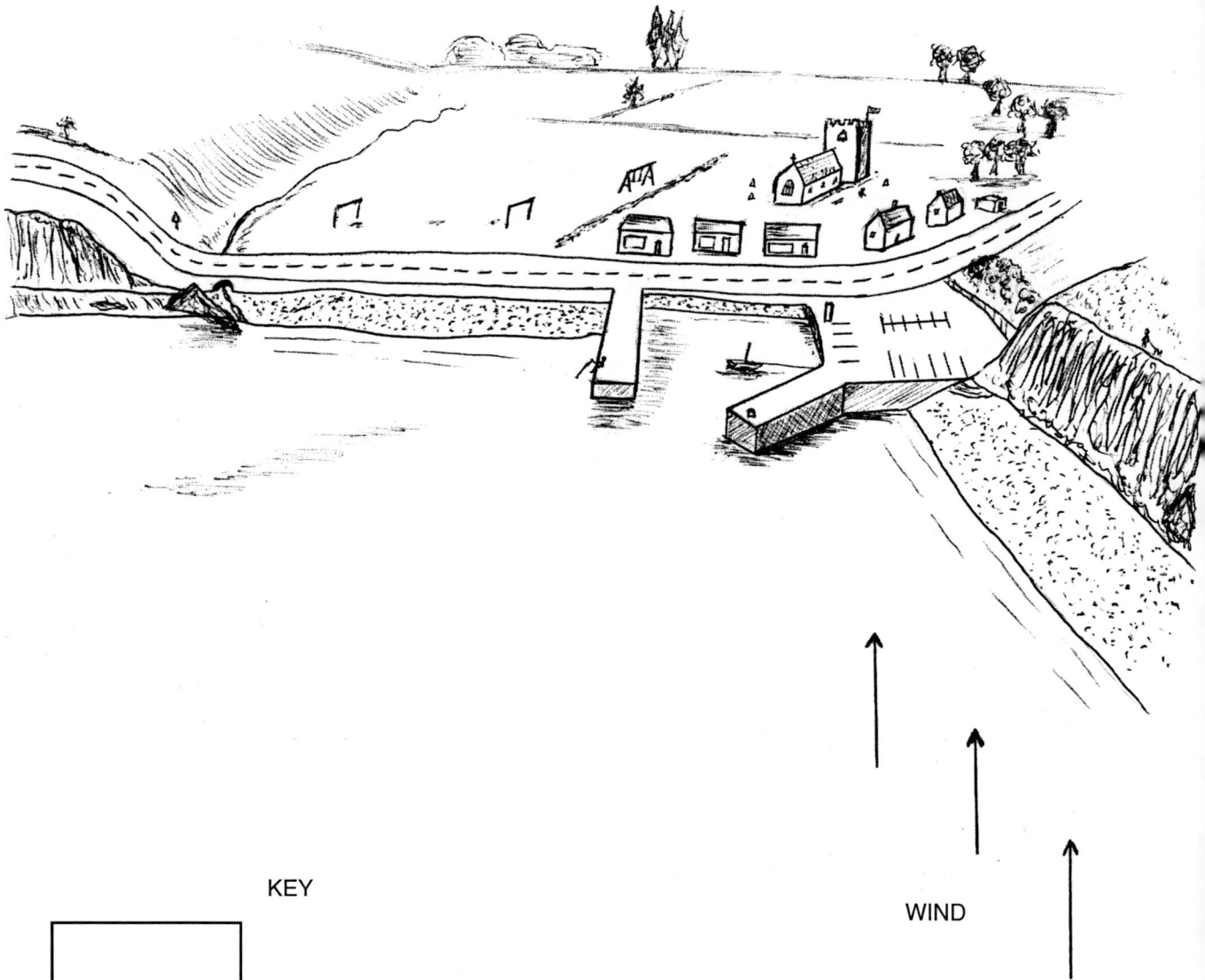

KEY

WIND

Chapter Nine

Using the Sea

Our seas and coasts are used for a wide range of activities, some of which are outlined below:

Fishing

This traditional industry has been a source of food and employment for millennia. Three types of nets are used: seine nets that operate like a giant purse; trawl nets that are dragged behind a boat, and drift or gill nets that ensnare the fish by their gills.

Only in recent years has there been a debate about preserving fish stocks and **over-fishing**. This has come about because of the efficiency of modern fishing methods. Within the European Union, the Common Fisheries Policy (CFP) aims to ensure we maintain **sustainable** fish stocks. To do this fishermen have to abide by quotas (agreed limits), including only landing catches of a certain size to conserve resources. The last decade has also seen the `decommissioning` (scrapping) of many fishing boats; in fact the UK fishing fleet has declined by over 30% since 1991.

In a similar way whaling is regulated by the International Whaling Commission. This body has 66 countries as members, including Britain and Japan.

1.   **What are the arguments for and against fishing quotas?**

2.   **Try to find out more about whaling and the significance of Japan being mentioned above.**

The Island of Lundy lies 19 km off the north coast of Devon. At just 5 km long, this small and remote island was originally the haunt of pirates. Its location in the Bristol Channel, as well as the jagged reefs just offshore, warrants it having two lighthouses. Since 1969 it has been owned by the National Trust and is administered by the Landmark Trust. There are no cars on the island, just a small village with an inn, a church and a thirteenth-century castle. Its stunning but dangerous coastline make it popular with visitors, who enjoy the wildlife above and below the waterline. The name comes from Lunde, the Old Norse word for a puffin: some of the birds still breed there.

Lundy is also in the middle of rich fishing grounds. It was therefore chosen as the UK's first **No-Take Zone**. This outlaws the fishing of any living creature, including fish, lobsters, crabs and scallops. It is recognised that other species will take longer to recover from over-fishing, such as sponges and soft corals indirectly affected by fishing. Established in 2003, it covers three-quarters of the eastern side of the island, and is the only statutory zone in the UK. It is monitored by scientists. Such no-take zones have been run successfully in other parts of the world - New Zealand has used them for ten years - but they still make up a tiny percentage of the world's oceans. However, a proposed Marine Bill could see the creation of more Marine Protected Areas.

Industry

Traditionally industries often have been located near the coast to enable water-borne transport of incoming raw materials and outgoing manufactured goods. **Canals**, such as the Manchester Ship Canal, put further cities within reach of the sea. In recent years nuclear power stations have been built on the coast to take advantage of plentiful cooling water.

There is always a risk of coastal **pollution**, either through accidents or illegal discharges of waste. For example, oil tankers are now forbidden from flushing out their tanks at sea, but the practice continues. Too much sewage flowing into the sea upsets the balance of oxygen and nutrients, and this can affect plankton and other creatures dependent on them. The disposal of nuclear waste sealed in large concrete flasks often takes place deep in the oceans, which may create problems for future generations.

Unsightly tourist hotels, resorts and other beach developments may also be considered a form of visual pollution. To this can be added increased levels of waste generated by them that often find their way into the sea. Even a large body of water such as the Mediterranean Sea is experiencing a worrying rise in the level of pollution because the narrow opening to the Atlantic Ocean through the Straits of Gibraltar limits the amount of water being replenished.

Links with History

S 3.   **Try to find out more about the Manchester Ship Canal, or a major canal such as the Suez or Panama Canals. Questions you might like to consider are:**

*   **Who built it?**

*   **When was it built?**

*   **What problems were encountered during construction?**

*   **How long is it?**

*   **By how much does it shorten the journey that has to be taken by ships?**

*   **Are there any locks?**

Minerals

The sea is also a source of mineral wealth. This ranges from salt, obtained by evaporating salt water, to the diamond fields on the beaches of southern Namibia in Africa, the richest source of gem diamonds in the world. Oil and gas are also extracted from the sea bed using huge rigs, such as those that operate in the North Sea.

Power

Various proposals have been put forward to harness the power of the sea, but to date there are few practical applications. One idea is to produce thermal energy using the temperature difference between surface water and deep water. Other schemes aim to exploit the power of the waves, tides or strong winds.

One of the latest proposals is to create a `Wave Hub` ten miles offshore from Hayle in Cornwall. The hub would act like a large electrical socket lying on the sea bed at a depth of 50 metres. Various wave power generators on or just below the surface would transmit power to the hub. From there it would be connected to the National Grid at Hayle via submarine cables.

The Wave Hub would enable various schemes to be tested in a site that has suitable sea conditions with waves reaching almost six metres. If it gains Government approval it could be in operation by the middle of 2007.

Links with Design Technology

4.   Try to design a system to produce power from the sea, either through the movement of the waves or the rise and fall of the tides. Remember, your ideas have to be practical, environmentally friendly, and not be a hazard to shipping.

Tourism

Many seaside towns, such as Blackpool or Bognor Regis, grew and prospered as tourist resorts during the Victorian and Edwardian periods. These have grown in importance since the Second World War now that people have longer annual holidays and more disposable incomes (a smaller proportion of wages is needed for basic needs such as food and housing, leaving savings for holidays). They may provide opportunities for a wide range of water sports, such as yachting, surfing, canoeing and diving.

Protecting People Using the Sea and Coasts

The task of protecting those who use the sea and coasts around the British Isles falls to the Royal National Lifeboat Institution (RNLI). In 2004 over 7,000 people were rescued at sea by RNLI crews, and the lifeboats had to be launched on 7,656 occasions. This voluntary organisation raises around £90 million to fund this service that operates 332 vessels. The latest Tamar class lifeboats are 16 metres in length and powered by two 1,000 horse-power turbo-charged diesel engines, have a top speed of 25 knots and a range of 250 nautical miles. Each vessel costs £2 million and carries a crew of seven, including a doctor. Other classes of lifeboat, as well as inshore rescue hovercraft and inflatable lifeboats, are also used by the service.

D 5. **There has long been a debate about whether the RNLI should be a charity or funded by the government. What do you think?**

6. **Look at Figure 1. Try to fill in the blanks which mark some of the main ports and harbours in the British Isles.**

S 7. **Make up a spreadsheet to set out the facts about lifeboats.**

Figure 1

Ports and Harbours

Fishing Ports ✖

Ferry Ports ✦

Navel Ports ⛴

S _____

Wick

S _____

Ullapool

F _____
Peterhead

A _____

Rosyth

Glasgow

N _____

Whitby

S _____

B _____

Hull   G _____

Belfast

F _____

L _____

Felixstowe

H _____

C _____

M _____

H _____

S _____   D _____

Poole   Folkestone

P _____

Weymouth

P _____

Newlyn   F _____

87

Case Study - The Port of Dover

The Port of Dover caters for a wide variety of needs, from cross-Channel services, cruising, freight, yachting and leisure craft. A hugely busy port, much of today's harbourside facilities have been built on reclaimed land fronting the famous white cliffs.

Freight is the commercial transportation of goods. The Port of Dover has eight roll-on/roll-off (known as Ro-Ro) ferry berths and a fast berth with a power mooring system. Despite the opening of the Channel Tunnel in 1993, Dover is still the country's leading ferry freight operator: in 2004 nearly two million lorries used the port, and this remains their core business.

Having no locks, and not being dependent on tides, Dover's **cargo** terminal operates around the clock. It handles the collection, storage and distribution of fresh, perishable goods such as fruit and vegetables, as well as bulk cargoes including grain and aggregates. The port also has a marshalling area for containers. These large, standardized boxes are ideal for **trans-shipment**, the direct transfer from one form of transport to another, such as ship to lorry - or even `slave-lorry` for the Channel crossing. Dover acts as a **break-point**, the point at which the journey has to be broken to change from one means of transport to another.

The Port of Dover is ideally situated for **cruise ships**, either sailing between southern and northern Europe, or as a port of embarkation for cruises to Scandinavia and the Baltic Sea. In 1996 the first of two dedicated cruise terminals was opened. Now Dover is one of northern Europe's busiest cruise ports, and able to cope with three arrivals and departures a day. Some cruise ships may carry over 2,000 passengers. Terminal 2 was opened in 2000 and, like Terminal 1, has a large lounge, check-in facilities, a baggage floor and a covered walkway providing all-weather access to the ships.

Dover is the gateway to the continent for many **passengers**, offering the shortest crossing to France. The port handled 14.3 million passengers and 4.5 million vehicles in 2004. Five ferry companies operate from here, using traditional ferries as well as jumbo catamarans. Hoverspeed's two 38-knot Seacats make the fastest sea crossing from Dover to Calais in just under one hour, and can carry 650 passengers and 140 cars or vans.

To cater for **yachts and leisure craft** there is also a marina with just over 400 berths, as well as all the facilities yachtsmen might need, from fuelling points to a boatyard that is able to store over 80 boats.

All these activities need support. Located in the marina, Dover has its own lifeboat station, opened in 2000. Security is also important: Port of Dover Police maintains a 90-strong force based in their own police station in Eastern Docks. They work closely with Customs and Immigration.

7. Why do you think the Port of Dover is so important?

8. What other types of transport also compete for Port of Dover's trade?

9. How does the Port of Dover compare with Falmouth Docks mentioned in the Case Study in Chapter 6?

10. Make up a spider diagram to show the main types of service offered by the Port of Dover. Choose a ship or something similar to go in the centre of your diagram, and brief headings and pictures around the outside to illustrate each facility.

11. What are some of the advantages of using containers to transport goods?

Use the map (Figure 2) page 90, to answer the following questions:

12. (a) If you had a yacht and wished to be able to put it to sea at any time, where would be the best place to moor it?

    (b) Why?

13. Why do you think the Port Control Building is located where it is?

14. What is the purpose of the Southern Breakwater?

15. Using the blank key provided on Figure 2, colour different parts of the map to show the various activities indicated.

90

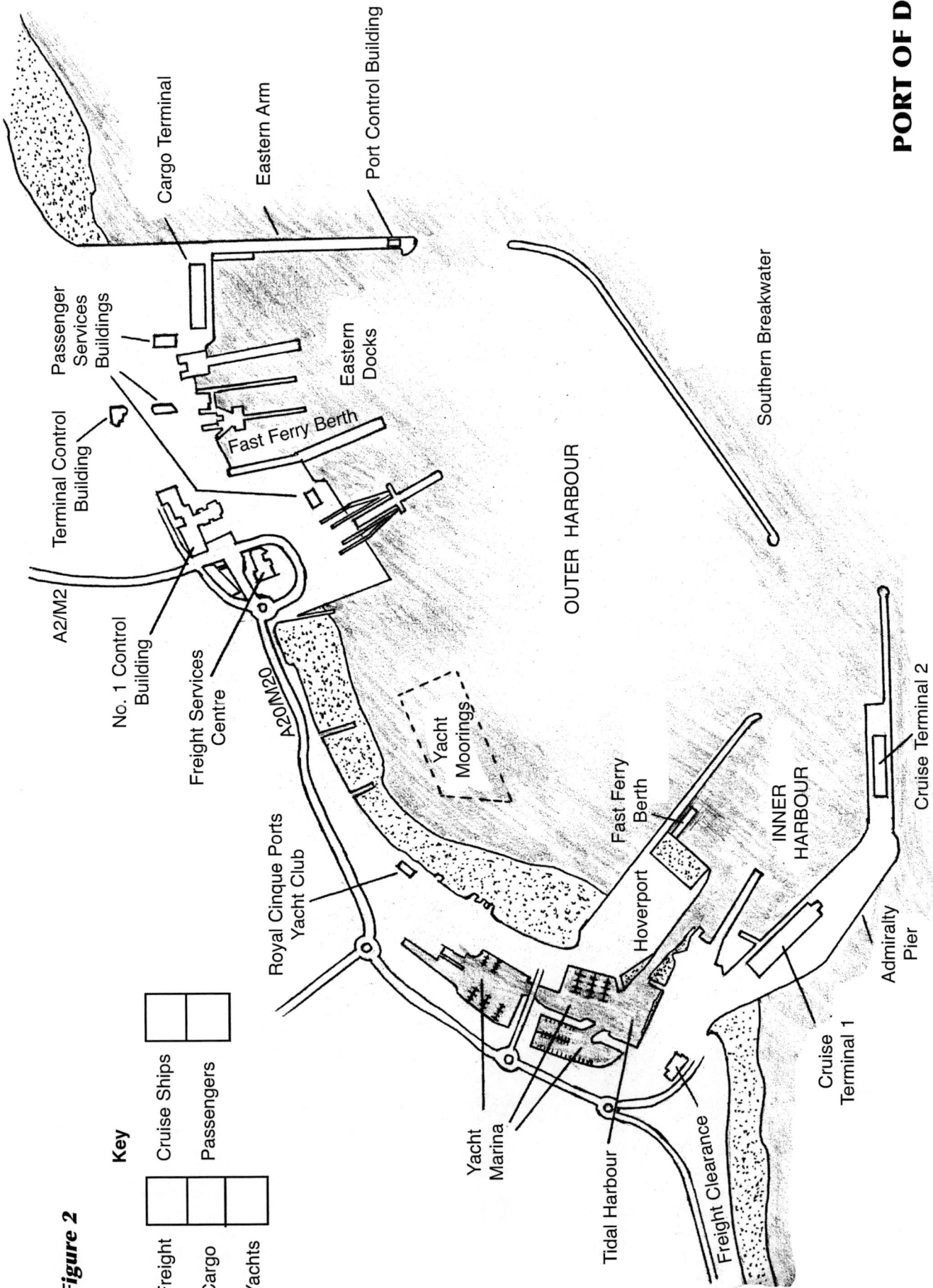

PORT OF DOVER

Figure 2

Key

Cruise Ships

Passengers

Freight

Cargo

Yachts

Cargo Terminal

Eastern Arm

Port Control Building

Passenger Services Buildings

Terminal Control Building

A2/M2

No. 1 Control Building

Freight Services Centre

A20/M20

Royal Cinque Ports Yacht Club

Fast Ferry Berth

Eastern Docks

OUTER HARBOUR

Southern Breakwater

Yacht Moorings

Fast Ferry Berth

Hoverport

INNER HARBOUR

Admiralty Pier

Cruise Terminal 2

Cruise Terminal 1

Yacht Marina

Tidal Harbour

Freight Clearance

Links with History

The Port of Dover has a fascinating history. It dates back to at least Roman times, when it was known as Dubris. During Saxon times the town joined up with the neighbouring ports of Hythe, Romney, Hastings and Sandwich for mutual protection against raids under what was known as the Cinque Ports. The port is also overlooked by the impressive twelfth and thirteenth-century castle. The four hundredth anniversary of the royal charter issued by King James I to establish a harbour board to maintain, administer and improve the port will be celebrated in 2006.

16. **Try to find out more about:**

    (a) **The Cinque Ports and their links with the Royal Navy,**

or

    (b) **The significant rôle Dover Castle and the underground tunnels have played in our history, even during World War II.**

17. **How do you think the Port of Dover's 400th anniversary should be celebrated?**

Chapter Ten

A Global Picture

From space, planet Earth mainly appears blue, as the seas and oceans cover three-quarters of the surface (the land surface is 149 million km², while water covers 361 million km²). Near the edges of the continents is a shallower area of sea known as the **continental shelf** (or euphotic zone). Sunlight can penetrate to the bottom of the shelf, so there is abundant sea life here.

Figure 1

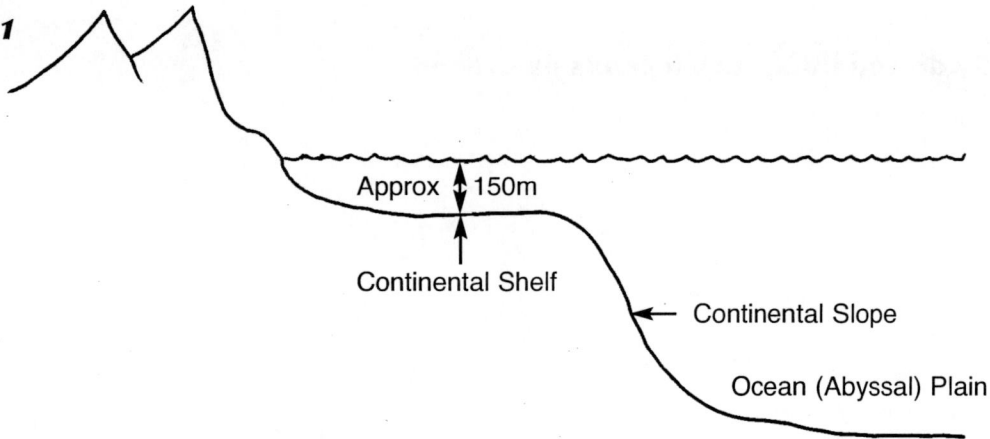

Beyond the continental shelf the ocean plain is undulating, with peaks like mountains, some breaking the surface as islands, and deep canyons or trenches. The deepest region is the Mariana Trench in the Pacific Ocean at 11,033 metres in depth.

It is now accepted that the earth's surface is divided up into tectonic plates, much like the broken shell of a hard-boiled egg, and the edges of many of these are found here. As these plates slip sideways against each other, or pull and push as they try to adjust their positions, underwater volcanoes and earthquakes often occur. The lava may create new land, such as the Hawaiian Islands, and in the warm, shallow seas these islands can be fringed by coral reefs or may form atolls if the island is later submerged. These underwater disturbances can also create large waves called **tsunami**, like the one that struck in the Indian Ocean on 26 December 2004.

Even though the temperature of the sea drops as the depth increases, the amount of light decreases and the water pressure rises, some creatures are able to live at the bottom of the deepest oceans. It remains a difficult area for man to reach, and we know less about the depths and the creatures that inhabit them than we do about the surface of the moon.

1.   Try to find out about mythical sea creatures such as mermaids and the Kraken.

2.   Why do you think such legends developed?

Ocean currents move in regular directions, generally rotating clockwise in the Northern Hemisphere and anticlockwise below the Equator. Some currents are cold, while others are warm. The Gulf Stream (and later the North Atlantic Drift) flows across the Atlantic Ocean from the Gulf of Mexico bringing warmer water to our shores than we would otherwise expect at our latitude. It also has a moderating effect on our climate. There is a fear that if global warming continues, causing the polar ice to melt and cold water to drift south, it could lead to the Gulf Stream changing course. This would result in the climate of the UK becoming colder rather than warmer, and we would experience harsher winters.

The seas and oceans affect our **weather** in other ways. As the sun shines, the land heats up more quickly than the sea, but the land also cools more quickly and the sea retains its warmth for longer. This is why a swimmer may be shocked by how cold the sea is on a hot day in June, while in September the sea may still feel relatively warm. The difference may also cause sea breezes to be generated on hot summer days as warm air rises off the land, drawing in cool, misty breezes from the sea.

Greenhouse gases, such as carbon dioxide (CO_2), help trap the heat from the Sun inside the atmosphere. Increased levels of greenhouse gases created by industry, power stations, cars, aeroplanes and so on are contributing to global warming.

Today the Greenland ice cap is over 3 kms thick and contains 10% of the world's water. If CO_2 emissions continue to grow and this ice melts we could expect sea levels to rise by seven metres. This would have severe consequences for many of the world's large cities, including London (see Case Study, Chapter 9) and Venice.

Case Study - The City of Venice, Italy

Venice, at the head of the Adriatic Sea, was originally built on 118 small islands. It is still a city that lives by water; there are no roads or cars so goods travel by barges and people by foot, vaporetto (water bus) or traditional gondolas. From humble beginnings when people sought sanctuary on the mud flats of the lagoon, and all building materials had to be transported there by boat, a majestic city emerged that was for a long time the greatest sea power in the world.

Figure 2 - General Location Map

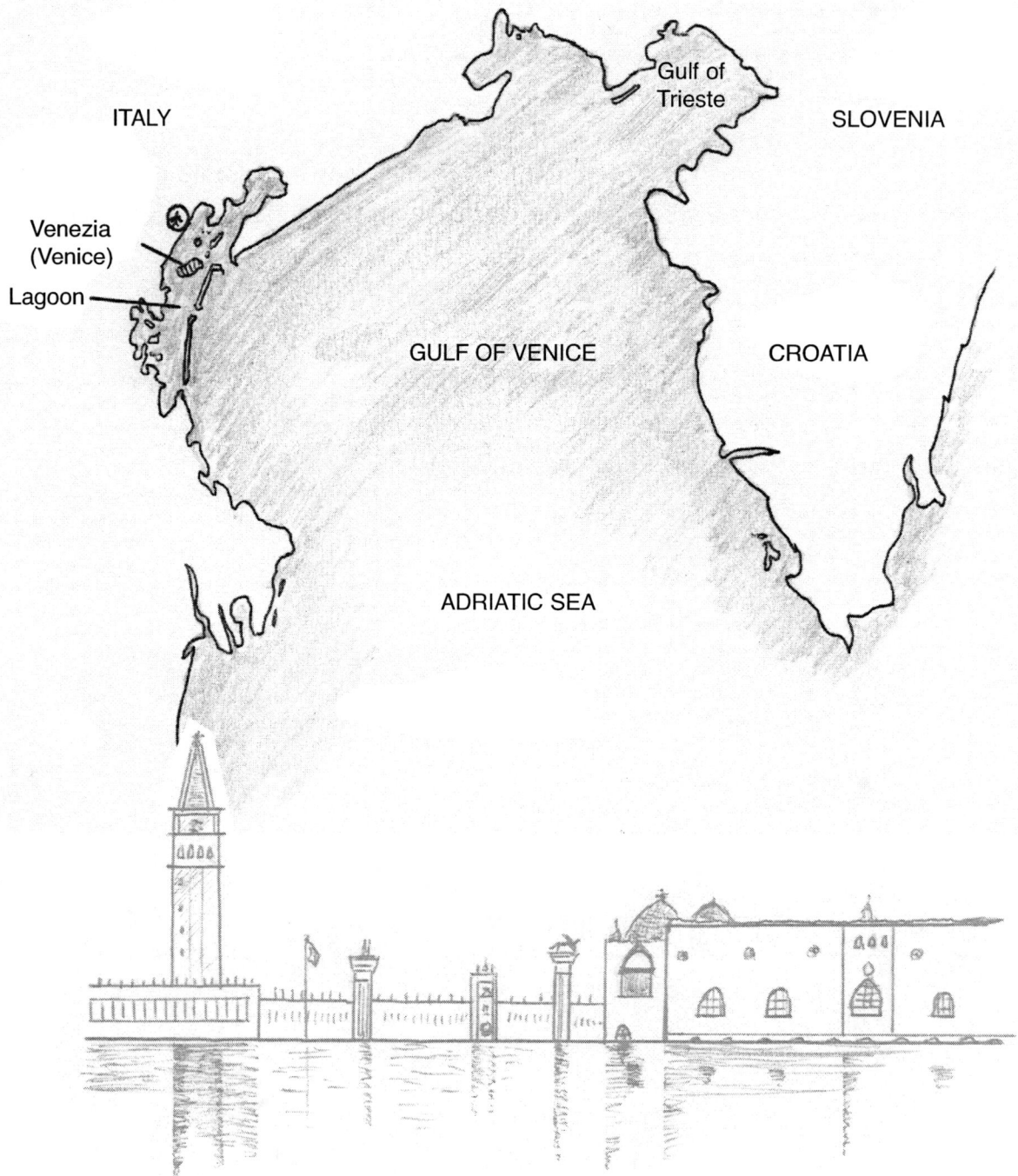

However, in modern times the sea has been trying to re-claim the city for its own. Venice is slowly sinking while, as we have seen, sea levels are rising. In 1966 it was inundated when the water in the lagoon rose by nearly two metres above the mean sea level, an occurrence known by Venetians as `aqua alta`. A programme was put in place to restore the magnificent buildings and works of art displayed in them, yet the underlying problem remains. Flooding is now not only a regular problem, it is becoming more frequent. Even when not flooded, the high tides often rise above the stone foundations of the buildings, harming the porous brickwork and limestone of the walls. The canals are regularly dredged to try to help the situation, but more drastic - and expensive - measures are needed.

It has been recognised that one of the problems that has caused the rate of subsidence (sinking) of around 100 mm per century to increase, has been the extraction of water from deep beneath the ground on the nearby mainland to serve industries there. Although this had stopped by the 1980s, the problem it created has continued. A suggestion has been made to replace the water by pumping sea water to a depth of 700 metres down 12 bore holes. It has been argued that if this was done constantly for the next ten years then Venice would rise by 30 cms. Other experts are sceptical of this scheme, saying that the city could rise unevenly, doing even more damage.

Other proposals have been more conventional and aim to protect the city during high tides. A £1.6 billion scheme is now about to start to build giant floodgates to protect the lagoon, similar to the Thames Barrier (see Case Study, Chapter 8). The `Moses Project` will use a line of 79 inflatable gates to stop the water flowing into the lagoon through its three inlets. Each gate will be 20 metres wide and 20 - 30 metres high when raised, but will fold flat on the sea bed like the Thames Barrier when not in use. When needed air will be pumped into the gates, causing one end to rise to form a dam. However, again the scheme has had its critics. Some are concerned about the effect on the city's drainage system and the danger of a build up in the levels of pollution. Others argue it will disrupt seaborne trade, which is certainly the case during the six to eight years it will take to construct it.

S **3.** **Which of the proposals do you favour and why?**

D **4.** **Try to find out more about Venice to answer the question, is the city worth saving, or are people just trying to delay the inevitable?**

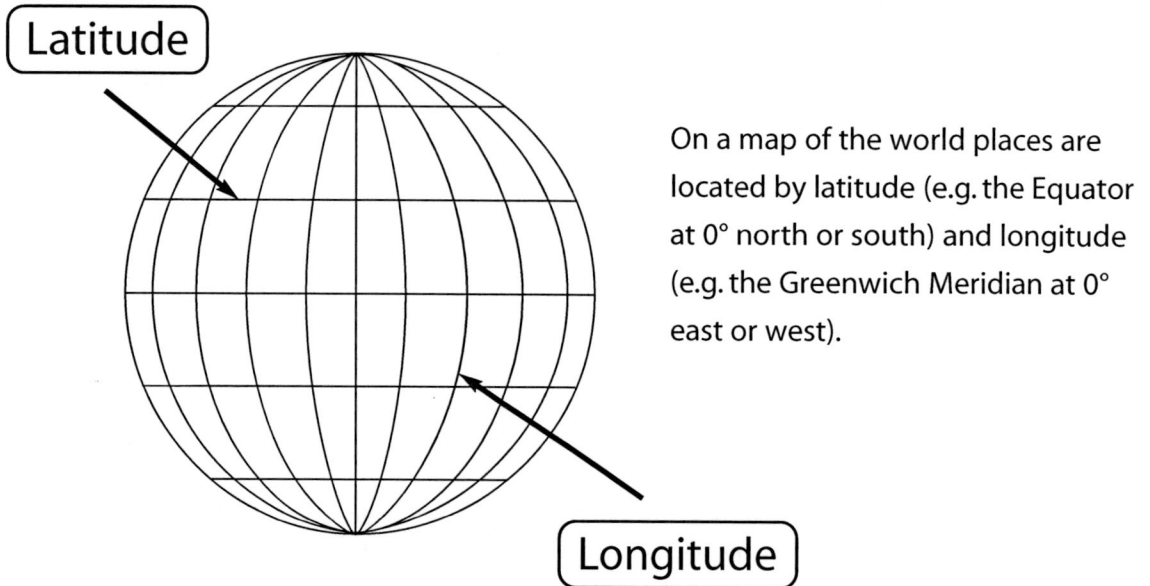

Latitude

Longitude

On a map of the world places are located by latitude (e.g. the Equator at 0° north or south) and longitude (e.g. the Greenwich Meridian at 0° east or west).

5. **Find the following examples of coastal features on a world map, using their co-ordinates.**

Tip: using an atlas, find the general location on a map of the world. Then look up the exact position on the most suitable map of that area.

A 1) Bay of _____ - 46° N 4° W

2) Straits of _____ - 35° 55' N 5° 40' W

3) Dutch Polders (below sea level) - ___° 30' N ____° 0' E

4) Cape _____ - 55° 50' S 67° 30' W

5) Cape York _____, Australia - 12° 0' S 142° 30' E

6) _____ Sea - 15° 0' N 75° 0' W

7) Gulf of _____ - 27° 0' N 111° 0' W

8) _____ Islands - 0° 0' N 91° 0' W

9) Suez Canal - ___° 58' N ___° 31'E

10) _____ Archipelago - 2° 30' S 150° 0'E

B **Plot the above places on a world map.**

$\mathrm{D}^{\!\!\!,\!\!\!,}\,$ c **Extension Work**

(a) Isthmus of _____ - 8° 49' N 79° 25' W

(b) _____ Passage - 58° 0' S 67° 0' W

(c) _____ Trench - 11° N 143° E

(d) _____ _____ Bight - 33° 30' S 130° 0' E

(Bight means _____)

(e) _____ Channel - 17° 30' S 42° 30' E

D **Try to identify these additional examples:**

(a) Straits of _____ - (Between England and France)

(b) _____ Canal - (Saves making a long trip around South America)

(c) _____ da _____ - (Remote island in South Atlantic Ocean)

(d) _____ Channel - (The French call it La Manche)

(e) M_____ - (Large island off Africa)

E **Colourful Waters**

(a) _____ Sea - North of Turkey

(b) _____ Sea - North of Arkhangelsk, Russia

(c) _____ Coast - Eastern Australia or West Africa

(d) _____ Sea - West of Saudi Arabia

(e) _____ Coast - West Africa

(f) _____ Sea - West of Korea

F **Historical Links - Place Names**

Drake Passage, South America

Straits of Magellan, South America

Hudson Bay, North America

Tasman Sea, Australasia

Cook Islands, Oceania

Amundsen Sea, Antarctica

Ross Sea, Antarctica

Try to find out why some of these places are named after these people.

S **6.** **Revision. Referring to previous chapters if necessary, fill in the spaces of the Coasts Jigword below:**

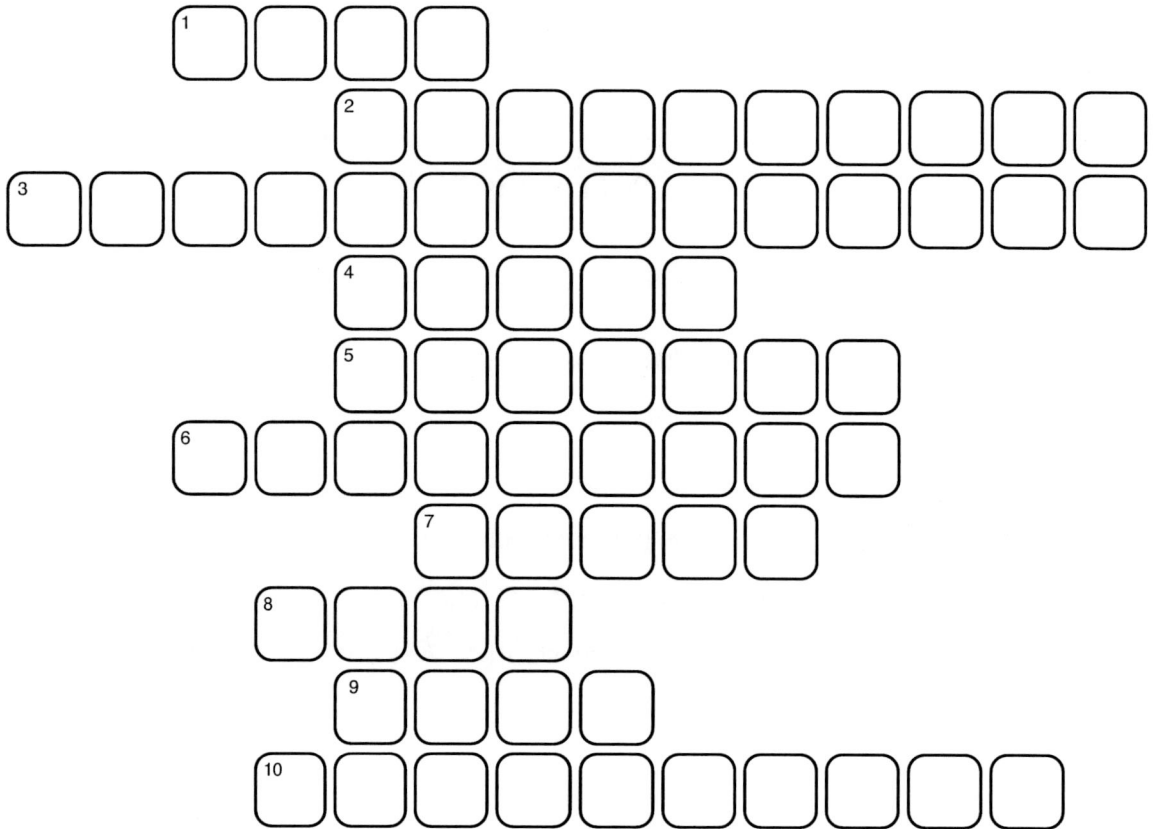

1. This is often the main material found on a beach.

2. Used to protect the coast.

3. The movement of eroded material from one place to another.

4. An indentation near the base of a cliff.

5. An example of a flooded coastline.

6. Land sticking out into the sea.

7. The regular rise and fall in sea level.

8. Formed by longshore drift.

9. A large, predictable wave created by tides.

10. A modern way of carrying goods; enables easy trans-shipment.

Answers

Chapter 1

1. The **Pacific Ocean** has the larger fetch because the winds have a much greater distance to cross.

2. The swash will carry sand and pebbles up the beach while backwash drags it back down again. As this happens the material will be eroded by this action.

3. The undertow will be formed by the circular movement of the water creating a current of water back out to sea. This can be dangerous for bathers as they can be dragged out to sea if they are not careful.

4. (a) Answers as diagram, Figure 2.

    (b) The best surf waves will be created by a flat or gentle slope where the wave is formed some distance off shore, affording a longer ride. In the second diagram the breakers form too late, while on a very steep beach they don't break cleanly at all.

Chapter 2

1. Figure 4 - Wave-Cut Platform

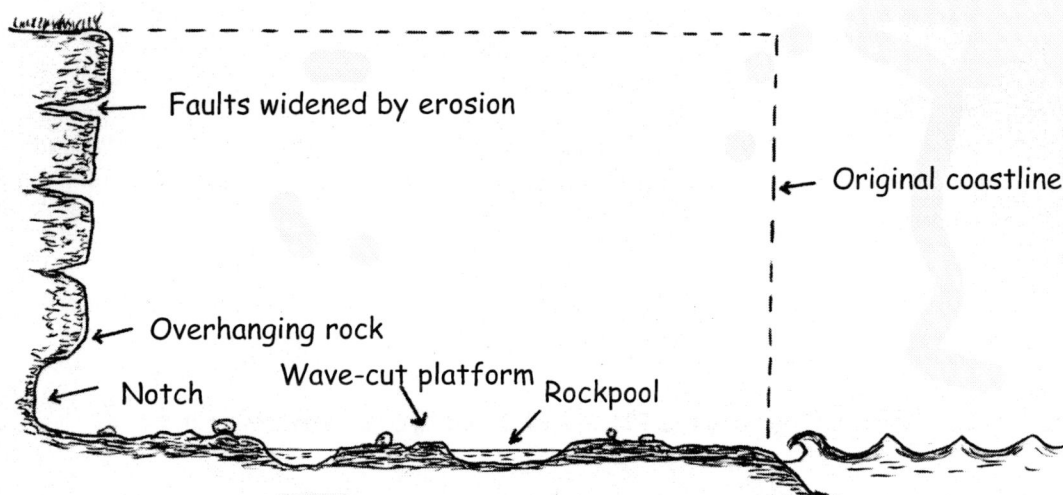

2. An area of hard rock may be **eroded** less quickly than the softer rock around it, leaving a **headland**. However, this may still have fissures, faults or weaknesses that will be eroded to form **caves**. On rare occasions a natural tunnel may be created, forming a **blowhole** that allows an incoming wave to shoot up in a fountain of water.

    Over time the sea may break through the back of the cave, forming an **arch**. When this natural bridge or lintel collapses a column of rock called a **stack** will be left. A small stack is known as a **stump**.

    The rate of erosion will depend on the **type** of rock that forms the cliff, and the power of the **waves**. This in turn may be influenced by the tides, prevailing **wind** and the fetch.

3. The highest sea cliffs in mainland Britian area at **Cape Wrath**, Scotland.

4. The nearest town to Beach Head is **Eastbourne**.

5. The cliffs face the **English** Channel and face **south**.

6. **Beachy Head lighthouse** stands at the base of the cliffs.

7. The cliffs at Beachy Head can be described as **porous**, **chalk**, **soft** and **tall**.

8. Large landslides may become more frequent because of more **extreme weather** conditions, as well as **rising sea levels** due to global warming.

9. **Walkers** are in danger, **buildings**, as well as **things beneath the cliffs**. Also, it is an indication of growing climate change that could have other repercussions.

10. Points to consider are the changes to well known coastal features. The changes may be caused by Man's effect on the environment. Landslides pose **a danger to people, animals, buildings, etc.**

Chapter 3

1. The pebble will be **moved up the beach at an angle** by the swash, then directly **back down by the backwash at 90 degrees to the shoreline**, so each wave is moving it along the beach.

2. On Figure 2 the sand and pebbles will move **from west to east**, and will continue to do so for as long as the wind blows in that south-westerly direction.

3. The movement could stop **if the wind ceased**, or be **reversed** if it changed to a south-easterly breeze.

4. Longshore drift is both a process of **erosion** and **deposition**. The eroded material will be transported, then dropped (deposited) elsewhere - see Chapter 4.

5. Longshore drift is a problem, for **sand is being removed from beaches**. They could eventually disappear entirely. Also, the sand has to go somewhere, and could be **swept in to harbours or cause dangerous reefs to form.**

6. Dismiss fans, teams of bulldozers, etc., as being impracticable. The best answer is to use groynes.

Chapter 4

1. The beach material ranges from **small pebbles** in the west **to large cobbles** in the east.

2. How the beach material is sorted depends on **longshore drift** and the strength of the **currents**.

3 The area is dangerous for swimming because of the **strong currents** along this stretch of coast.

6 (a) This could lead to a study of the dissolution of the monasteries under Henry VIII, and the effect of this on local communities and their activities, such as at Abbotsbury.

(b) Fleet Lagoon was used for testing some of the bouncing bombs used by the Dam Busters during World War Two. An example can be seen at Abbotsbury Swannery.

7

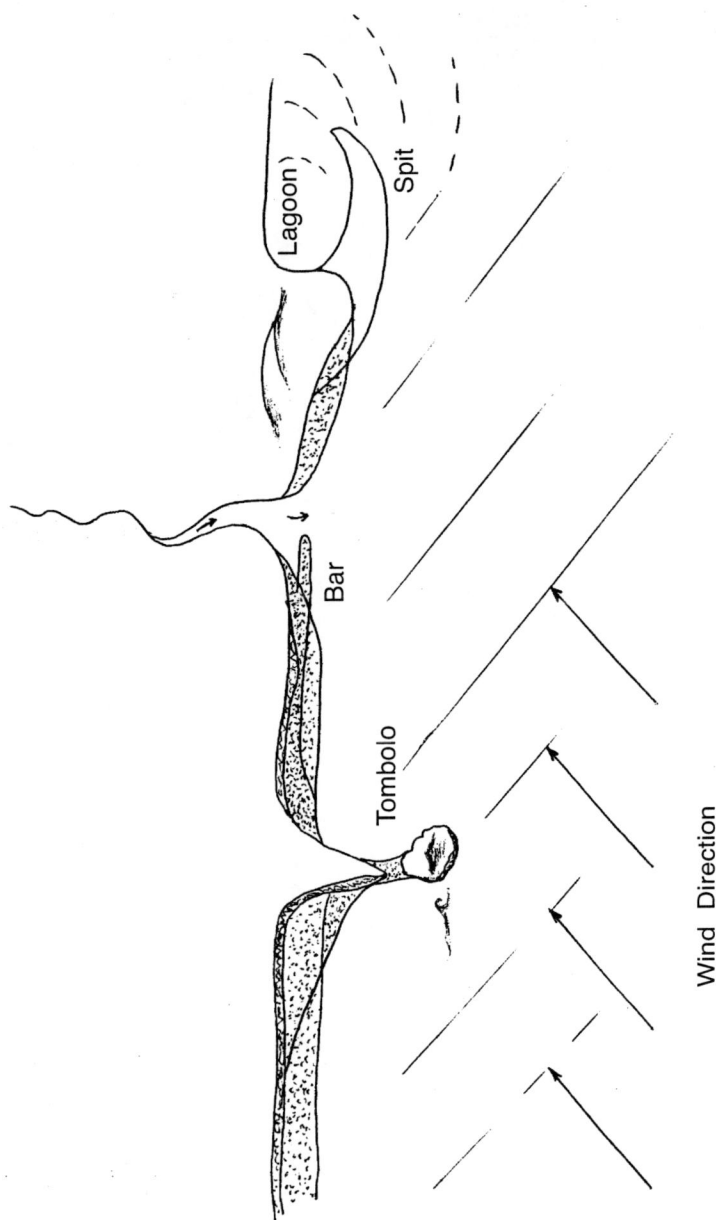

Figure 6 – Coastal Deposition Simulation

Figure 1

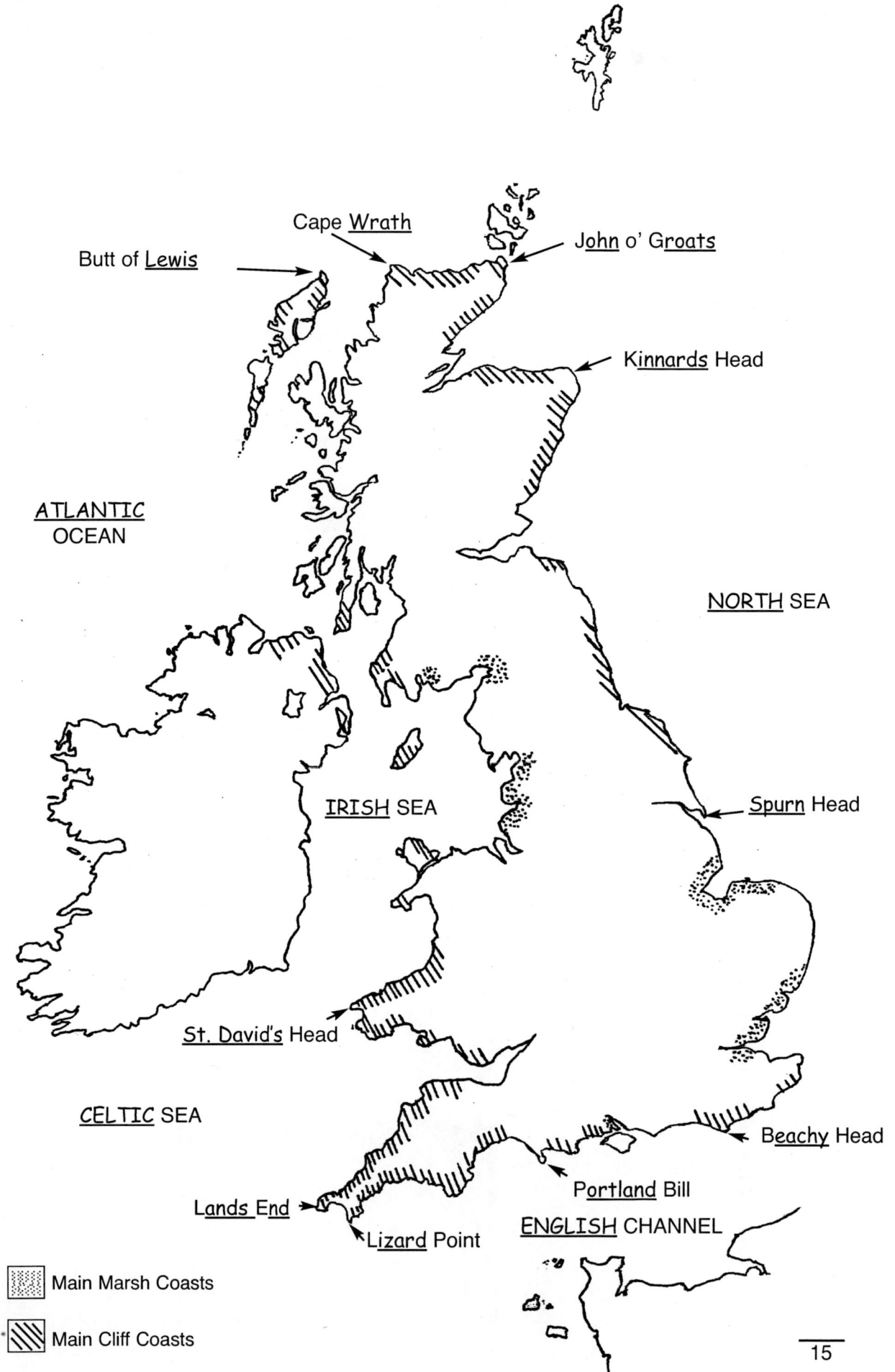

Butt of <u>Lewis</u>

Cape <u>Wrath</u>

John o' G<u>roats</u>

K<u>innards</u> Head

<u>ATLANTIC</u>
OCEAN

<u>NORTH</u> SEA

<u>IRISH</u> SEA

Spurn Head

St. <u>David's</u> Head

<u>CELTIC</u> SEA

<u>B</u>e<u>achy</u> Head

Lands <u>End</u>

<u>Portland</u> Bill

<u>Lizard</u> Point

<u>ENGLISH</u> CHANNEL

Main Marsh Coasts

Main Cliff Coasts

15

Chapter 5

1. A range of proposals, many fanciful, may be put forward. The simplest and cheapest remedy is to plant marram grass to stabilize the dunes.

2. **Advantages** of island life include a sense of independence, a remoteness from the hustle and bustle of urban life, and tax consessions on islands such as the Isle of Man and the Channel Islands. **Disadvantages** may include a feeling of isolation, distances and time taken to travel to centres of population, and the remoteness from facilities such as major hospitals or colleges and universities.

3.
Cliff Coastline	**Salt Marshes**
Cornwall	The Wash
The Mull of Kintyre	Essex
The Isle of Man	Morecambe Bay
Northumberland	
Cardigan, Wales	
Dover	
North Devon	

5. (c) There is probably **no need** for a further crossing at the present time. Other factors that would need to be considered are the cost of construction and maintenance, and how to **avoid impeding river traffic**.

6.

	Islands		**Inlets**
1	Shetland Is.	9	Moray Firth
2	Orkney Is.	10	Firth of Forth
3	Hebrides	11	Firth of Clyde
4	Isle of Man	12	Solway Firth
5	Anglesey	13	Bristol Channel
6	Isles of Scilly	14	The Wash
7	Isle of Wight	15	Thames Estuary
8	Channel Isles		

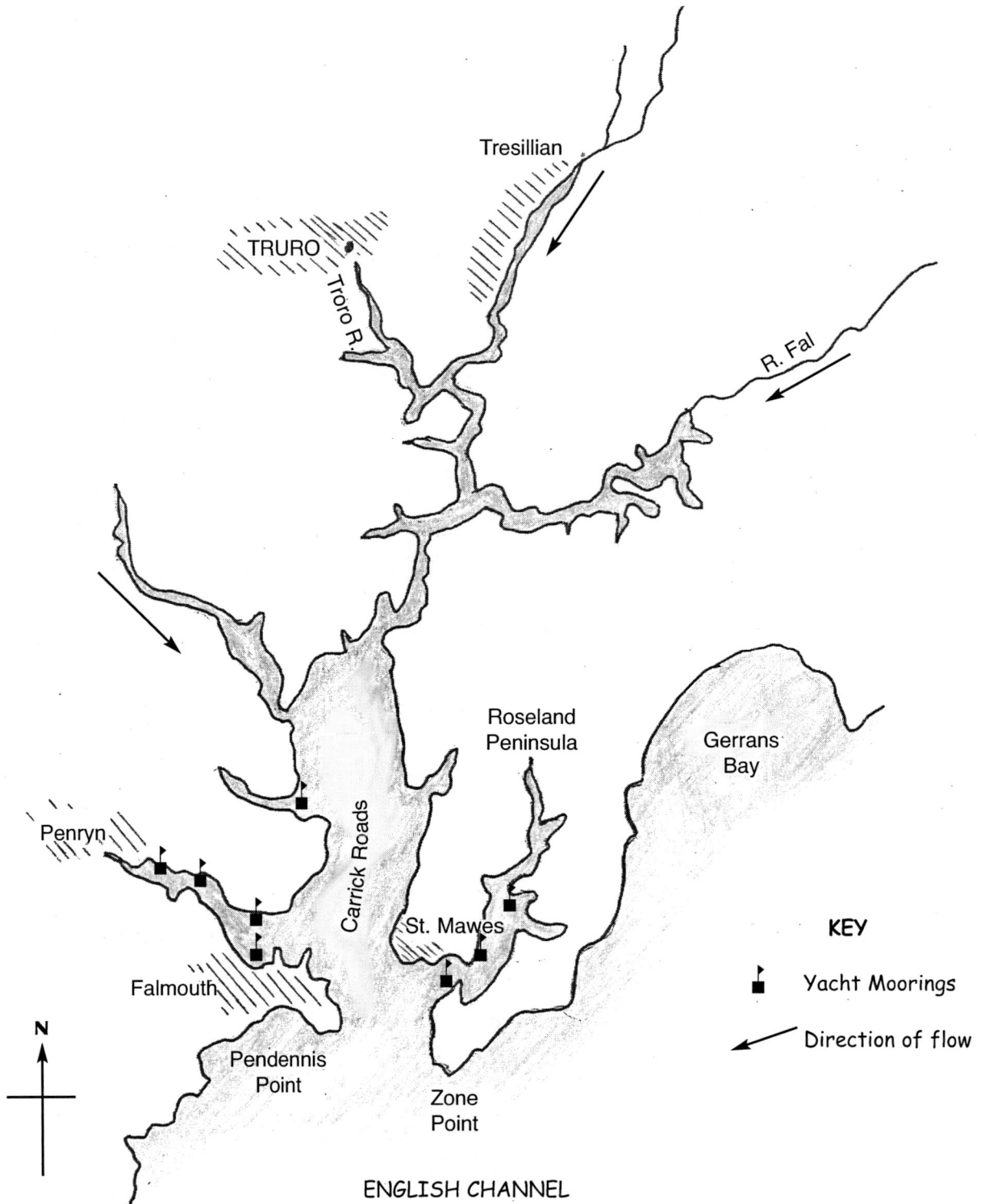

Chapter 6

Tresillian

TRURO

Troro R.

R. Fal

Roseland
Peninsula

Gerrans
Bay

Carrick Roads

Penryn

St. Mawes

KEY

■ Yacht Moorings

↙ Direction of flow

Falmouth

N

Pendennis
Point

Zone
Point

ENGLISH CHANNEL

1.   See Above.

2.   See Glossary.

3.   The Fal Estuary is **useful for boats**, but forms a natural **obstacle to land-borne transport** between the west and east. The main road to Falmouth from the east, the A39, runs through Truro and Penryn. However, the King Harry car ferry and a passenger ferry between St. Mawes and Falmouth cut journey times for people living on the Roseland Peninsula.

4.   An estuary or ria may be formed when a river valley is flooded by the sea when sea levels rise at the end of an ice age. It would be similar to Figure 3, but without being widened and deepened by glaciers.

5.   The Norwegian fjords were used by the Germans to harbour battleships such as the *Tirpitz*. This 42,000-ton vessel was moored in Altenfjord in September 1943 when it was famously attacked by two British midget submarines and put out of action with explosive charges.

Chapter 7

2.   The Broadlands are essentially a **man-made** environment. The Broads were created through **peat cutting**, the **water levels have been controlled, new species** such as coypu introduced, **water has been extracted** for homes and industry, and they remain important for **leisure activities**.

3.   **Rising sea levels**, and **increases in salinity** could mean that parts of the Broads will need to be abandoned to natural forces.

Chapter 8

1.   People choose to live close to the sea to enjoy the **views**; it is ideal for **hotels**; for **health benefits**; they often enjoy **high property values**; the family has lived there a long time; or they don't consider the risk to be significant.

3 (a) The storm beach suggests the coast here is subjected to a **regular assault by the sea**.
  (b) The wall is concave in shape to **dissipate the power of the sea** and **throw back the waves**.
  (c) The beach is **not ideal** for visitors as it has been formed **into steps by storms**, and also in places comprises of **large pebbles**.
  (d) If the sea wall was breached the low land and **houses behind the esplanade could be flooded**.

7.   When extreme tides are forecast the **gates of the barrier are revolved** from a horizontal position level with the cill to a vertical situation to form a dam.

8.   The Thames Barrier is likely to be operated **more frequently** in future if predictions of **higher sea levels** and increased high tides prove correct.

9.   **At the moment the Thames Barrier works well** as it protects London from flooding while river traffic is not affected. However, it is open to question **whether it will be adequate to meet predicted rises in sea levels**.

10. Examples of cities at risk include **Amsterdam**, **New York**, and **Venice** (see Chapter 10).

11. Possible solutions are:

Figure 3

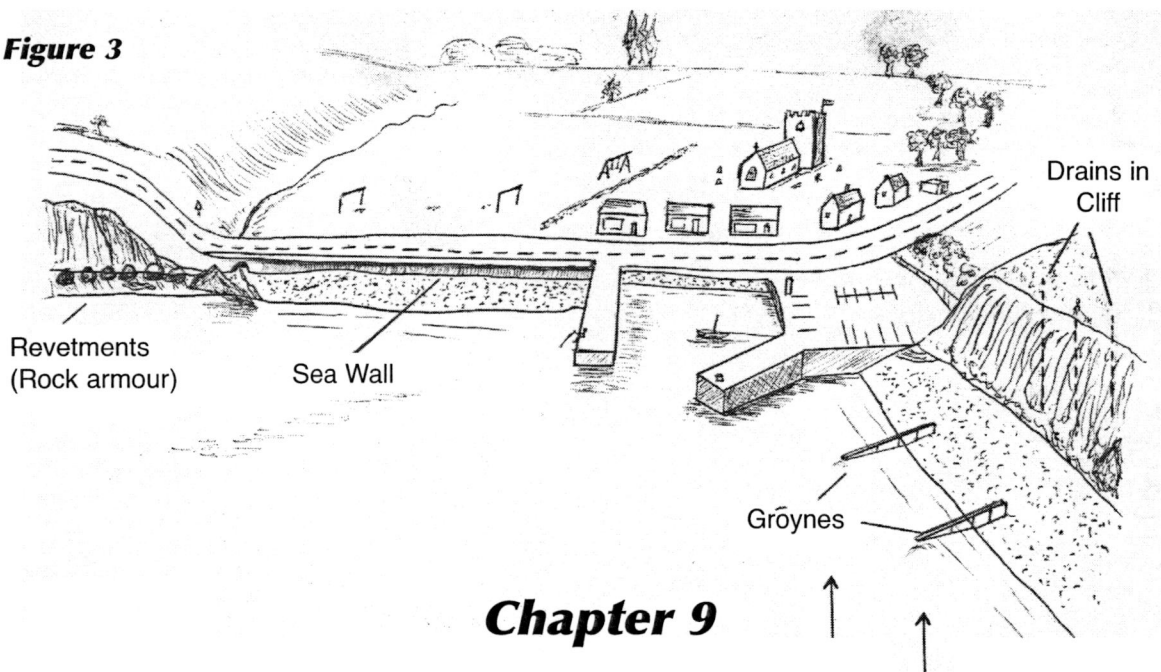

Revetments
(Rock armour)

Sea Wall

Drains in
Cliff

Groynes

Chapter 9

1.	Fishing quotas are designed to **protect fish stocks**. This is being achieved. However, many fishermen and their families have suffered from **loss of earnings** or even the **decommissioning** of their fishing boats.

5.	The RNLI themselves claim they offer a **better service now** than they would if they had to rely on government funding.

6.	See Figure 1 (next page)

7.	Many factors have led to Port of Dover's success: its **close proximity to the continent** has meant that historically it has been an important gateway into Britain; it enjoys **excellent transport links** such as roads, railways and the nearby Channel Tunnel; it is also relatively **close to the capital**, London. The port has also enjoyed **steady investmen**t to keep its facilities up-to-date and to cater for new technologies.

8.	Today Port of Dover has to compete with other transport systems, such as **railways** using the Channel Tunnel, as well as **aircraft**.

9.	Port of Dover is **a much bigger** facility than Falmouth Docks, and is able to **handle far more trade**. Falmouth's location in the extreme south-west has been both a help and a hinderance. Its sheltered position means that it is ideal for ship repairs and replenishing provisions.

11.	Some advantages of containers are:
	* They are **standard sizes** so are **easily trans-shipped**
	* They are **weather-proof**
	* They **can be refrigerated**
	* They are **secure**
	* They are **easily handled** with special cranes.

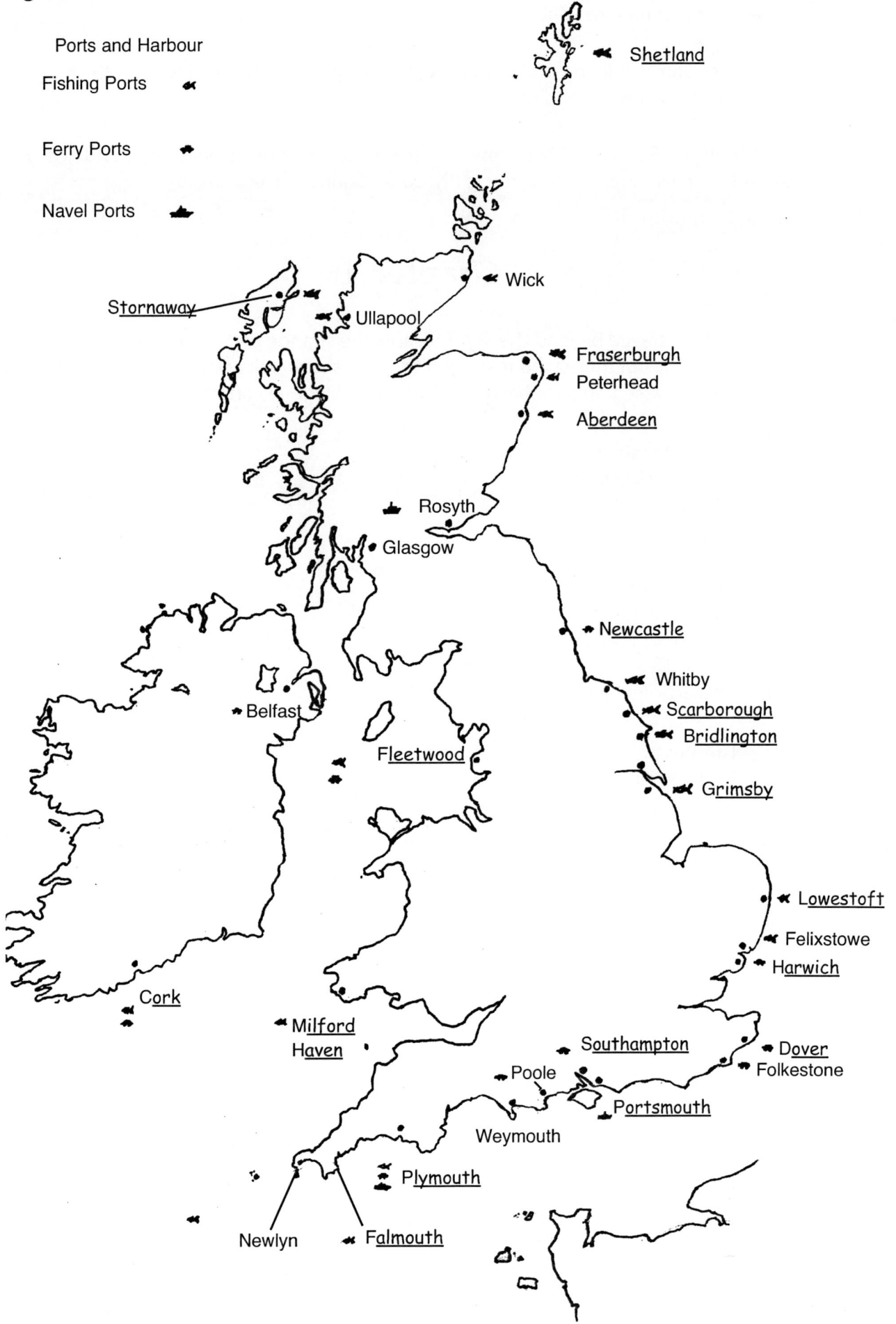

Figure 1

Ports and Harbour

Fishing Ports ᐊᐊ

Ferry Ports ᐊ

Navel Ports ᐼ

Shetland

Wick

Stornaway

Ullapool

Fraserburgh
Peterhead

Aberdeen

Rosyth

Glasgow

Newcastle

Whitby

Scarborough

Bridlington

Grimsby

Belfast

Fleetwood

Lowestoft

Felixstowe

Harwich

Cork

Milford
Haven

Southampton

Dover
Folkestone

Poole

Portsmouth

Weymouth

Plymouth

Newlyn

Falmouth

113

12 (a) The yacht moorings in the **outer harbour** would be the best choice.
(b) The other marinas are tidal.

13. The Port Control Building is able to **monitor vessels** entering and leaving the harbour from its position at the end of the Eastern Arm.

14. The Southern Breakwater helps **protect the outer harbour** from storms and heavy seas. (A similar breakwater protects Plymouth Sound in Devon.)

Chapter 10

2. Once sailors strayed beyond the sight of land, the strange and unexpected soon became the talk of those who managed to avoid shipwreck and returned to port. As stories were passed on tales became legends, and legends often accepted as fact.

5.

A
1. Bay of Biscay
2. Straits of Gibraltar
3. 52° 30' N 5° 0' E
4. Cape Horn
5. Cape York Peninsula, Australia
6. Caribbean Sea
7. Gulf of California
8. Galápagos Islands
9. 29° 58' N 32° 31' E
10. Bismarck Archipelago

C
(a) Isthmus of Panama
(b) Drake Passage
(c) Mariana Trench
(d) Great Australian Bight (A bight is a curving coastline)
(e) Mozambique Channel

D
(a) Straits of Dover
(b) Panama Canal
(c) Tristan da Cunha
(d) English Channel
(e) Madagascar

E
(a) Black Sea
(b) White Sea
(c) Gold Coast
(d) Red Sea
(e) Ivory Coast
(f) Yellow Sea

6.

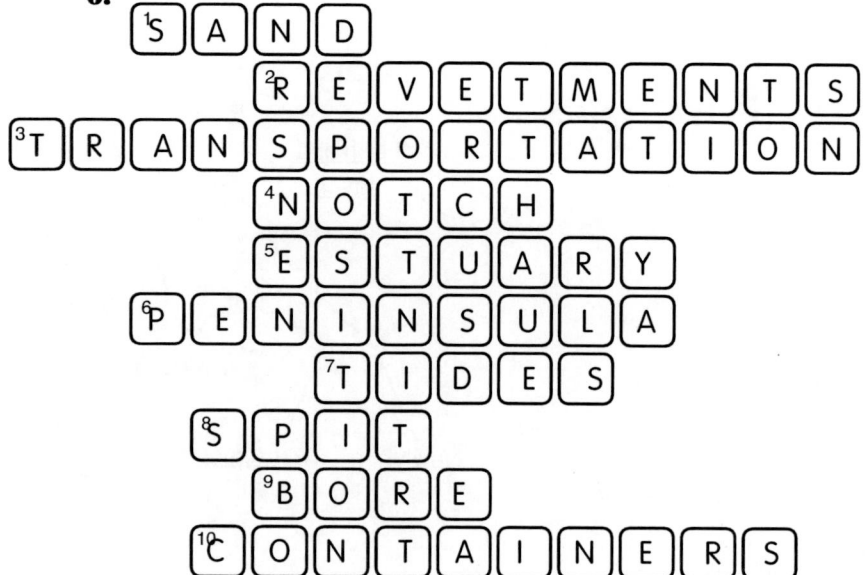

Glossary

Coasts

Arch - a curved natural bridge of rock formed by wave action.

Archipelago - a group of islands, or the sea containing them.

Backwash - water running back down a beach after a wave has broken.

Bay - a wide opening in the coast.

Beach - the shore, usually made up of sand and pebbles.

Beach feeding (or **beach nourishment**) - adding sand to replenish a beach.

Bight - a curving coastline.

Bore - a wave created in a river mouth by the tides.

Breaker - The motion of a wave as it curls over and crashes upon the shore.

Cave - a hollow made in the side of a cliff as a result of erosion.

Coast - the boundary between land and sea.

Constructive wave - a wave that adds material to a beach.

Continental Shelf - a shallower area of sea bed bordering the continents.

Crest - the top of a wave.

Deposition - dropping or depositing material such as sand.

Destructive wave - a wave that removes material from a beach.

Ebb - the outward movement of the tide.

Fetch - the distance across which waves travel unimpeded before making landfall.

Groynes - man-made structures to prevent longshore drift removing beach material.

Headland - a piece of land, usually of harder rock, left sticking out into the sea.

High water mark - the highest point the tide normally reaches.

Isthmus - a narrow stretch of land with sea on either side.

Lagoon - a sheltered area of shallow water.

Longshore drift - sand moved along a beach by a diagonal wave pattern.

Low water mark - the point reached by the lowest tides.

No-Take Zone - an area of sea inside which fishing is prohibited.

Notch - an indentation in a rock or cliff created at the greatest point of erosion by the sea.

Peninsula - a narrow strip of land almost surrounded by water.

Revetments - sea defences formed by large rocks that act like a sea wall.

Rock armour - large boulders placed at the foot of a cliff to protect it.

Salt marsh - marshy wetland flooded by salt water.

Sand dunes - mounds of loose sand.

Seaboard - American term for land bordering the sea; the coast.

Seafront - a built-up area facing the sea.

Sea bed - the land beneath the sea or ocean.

Shingle - coarse gravel found on beaches.

Spit - a tongue of sand created by longshore drift.

Stack - a large column of rock; the remnant of an arch or headland.

Storm surge - a sudden rush of water caused by storms or torrential rainfall.

Stump - a small rock standing above sea level; the remnant of a stack.

Swash - white, foaming water running up a beach after a wave has broken.

Tide - the rise and fall of sea level due to the attraction of the moon and sun.

Wave - the curving ridge of surface water.

Wave-cut notch - an area at the base of a cliff undercut by wave action (See notch).

Wave-cut platform - the flat area at the foot of a cliff worn back by concentrated wave action.

Wavelength - the distance from one wave crest to another.

General

Abrasion - erosion of a cliff caused by pebbles and rocks being thrown by the waves.

Aspect - the direction a feature is facing.

Attrition - erosion caused by rocks and pebbles colliding.

Break-point - the point at which a journey has to be broken to change from one means of transport to another.

Canal - a man-made waterway.

Chandler - a person or business that deals in ships' supplies.

Container - a large metal box of standard size used for the transport of goods.

Corrosion - the process by which salt and chemicals in sea water dissolve certain rocks.

Creek - a narrow inlet or bay.

Ecosystem - a community of plants, animals or sea creatures that are dependent upon the interaction of all the elements that make it up.

Embarkation - the boarding of a ship (or aircraft).

Fault - an area of weakness in a rock.

Freight - the commercial transportation of goods.

Ground water - water held in the surface soil.

Hydraulic action - erosion resulting from air being trapped in cracks in cliffs and compressed by the power of waves.

Ice cap - a mass of ice permanently covering an area of land.

Impermeable - rock that does not allow water to pass through it.

Merchant ship - a ship used to carry cargo; engaged in trade.

Navigable - where it is wide, deep and safe enough for a vessel to be used.

Packet ship - a ship used to carry messages, letters and parcels.

Permeable - rock that water can pass through or is able to penetrate along joints.

Pollution - harmful or undesirable substances damaging the environment.

Prevailing wind - the direction from which the wind most frequently blows.

Replenish - to restock with supplies, e.g. a ship before a voyage.

Source - the start of a river.

Sustainability - the ability for something to be maintained or replenished.

Transportation - the movement of beach material along the coast as the result of the action of waves.

Trans-shipment - The movement of goods from one form of transport to another, e.g. from a lorry to a ship.

Tributary - a small river that joins a larger one.

Tsunami - a large wave created by an earthquake, landslide or meteorite.

Weathering - the natural breakdown of rocks by rainwater, the sun, chemicals, plants or animals.